SEX OUTSIDE THE LINES

SEX OUTSIDE THE LINES

AUTHENTIC SEXUALITY IN A SEXUALLY DYSFUNCTIONAL CULTURE

CHRIS DONAGHUE, PHD

BenBella Books, Inc.
Dallas, TX

BenBella Books, Inc.
10300 N. Central Expressway
Suite #530
Dallas, TX 75231
www.benbellabooks.com
Send feedback to feedback@benbellabooks.com

Printed in the United States of America
10 9 8 7 6 5 4 3 2 1

Library of Congress Cataloging-in-Publication Data:
Donaghue, Chris.
Sex outside the lines : authentic sexuality in a sexually dysfunctional culture / Chris Donaghue.
pages cm
Includes bibliographical references and index.
ISBN 978-1-940363-78-3 (hardback) — ISBN 978-1-940363-88-2 (electronic) 1. Sex (Psychology) 2. Sex. 3. Sexual disorders. 4. Sex customs. I. Title.
BF692.D66 2015
306.77—dc23
2015011897

Editing by Erin Kelley
Copyediting by Oriana Leckert
Proofreading by Laura Cherkas and Brittney Martinez
Indexing by WordCo Indexing Services, Inc.
Cover design by Pete Garceau
Jacket design by Sarah Dombrowsky
Text design and composition by Aaron Edmiston
Printed by Lake Book Manufacturing

Distributed by Perseus Distribution
www.perseusdistribution.com

To place orders through Perseus Distribution:
Tel: (800) 343-4499
Fax: (800) 351-5073
E-mail: orderentry@perseusbooks.com

Think outside of the box…this is important if you want to make changes.

—Dr. Adrian J. Donaghue

One should always be in love. That is the reason one should never marry.

—Oscar Wilde

Nature is constructed, not discovered.

—Donna J. Haraway

The constraints imposed by social facts are invisible to us, unless we actively try to resist them.

—Emile Durkheim

Once you are Real you can't be ugly, except to people who don't understand.

—Margery Williams (*The Velveteen Rabbit*)

When a hundred men stand together, each of them loses his mind and gets another one.

— Friedrich Nietzsche

CONTENTS

INTRODUCTION

We live in a world where sex is under attack.

Though it's often been a cultural obsession through the ages, sex is constantly in our headlines, in the form of sex addiction, political sex scandals, high school kids sexting, college campus consent laws, and celebrity marriages, divorces, and cheating scandals. Sex has become a psychological police state: always under surveillance and framed as dangerous.

The topic of sex, even clinically and within academia, carries a stigma. Sexologist Betty Dodson wryly pointed out that "people who love and explore sex are no different from food connoisseurs, dedicated scientists, or other people who devote time to pursuing a particular interest. When I was an artist working long hours painting, I was admired and rewarded. Once I became interested in spending my time pursuing sex, I was labeled 'nymphomaniac' or, more recently, 'sex addict'" (Dodson, 1996, p. 56).

A healthy sex education would be honest, maybe even transgressive in our current societal climate, and would encourage people to free themselves of the shame created by their sexual desires. The ultimate goal of sex education should be to free our minds and bodies for pleasurable exploration, not further oppression and damage. My own clinical and academic training, especially within the sex addiction field, was rife with attempts at social control. The sex addiction treatment model shames non-normative sex acts, pornography, and masturbation. Its goal is to water down sex and keep it within committed relationships only, calling anything else "addiction." That's morality, not psychology. What I needed was a conversion from "sex addiction," which is sex-negative, to "sexology," which is sex-positive. I did not enter psychology and sexology to confine and control individuals via therapeutic oppression or to act as a judge, doling out punishment and shame. I entered this field to liberate people and to support their sustained health, both mental and physical.

This book is about destabilizing the sexual "norms" of Western society. Sex addiction therapies, sexual harassment, and sexual disorder diagnoses all create a paralysis around empowered and authentic sexuality. I strive to liberate people by helping them create their own spaces for the kinds of sex they want to have. The goal of my work is to create space for more sexual-relational options and visions of sexual "health." Current self-designated "experts" allow their sex-hating narratives to cloud their critical thinking. It's easier to stick with the story that sex is shameful. Most therapists and psychiatrists have no formal sex therapy training, yet they work with couples and individuals on sexual "dysfunction" on a regular basis.

We do not need to be more liberal within current concepts; we need to be more inventive by creating new sexual values that are sustainable and relevant to our current and future sexual-relational systems. We must not allow our sex lives to be directed by sex-negative policing.

Language is typically the first site of regulation and shaming. As Camille Paglia said, "Words must never be policed. Whatever good some people feel may be gained by restriction on speech, it is enormously outweighed by the damage done to any society where expression is restricted" (1994, p. 50). This is especially true of sexual language, which is policed and prohibited in our society more than any other kind of expression, with the possible exception of hate speech. That comparison should illuminate how our culture truly views sex.

To recover, a person must first acknowledge they have been sexually repressed or restrained, then learn what it means to move beyond that. We will know sex is free when sex work is safe and legal, sex addiction as a clinical issue no longer exists, and fetishes are not pathologized as unhealthy or something of which people need to be "cured."

Sex Outside the Lines works to rescue sex from the oppressive and violent place where it currently exists, within psychological discourses, media presentations, institutional policing, and interpersonal practices. Our current knowledge, theories, and presentations of sex and relationships are created by people who are afraid of sexuality. These theories continue to hinder healthy sex and sustainable relationships. New models for sexuality and relationship are desperately needed, as evidenced by the statistical view of modern American society:

- Highest rate of singledom
- High rate of divorce
- In 50 percent of all relationships one or both partners have cheated
- The majority of U.S. households are unmarried households
- The marriage rate has been declining for the past one hundred years
- More couples with kids cohabitating but not getting married
- 45 percent of the adult population is unmarried
- Unmarried women are the fastest-growing demographic
- Single women do more than 30 percent of adopting

All these problems stem from one thing: our societal fear of and distaste for sexuality. It's time to confront some facts:

Marriage doesn't work for everyone and is no longer needed to signify love and commitment, gender is no longer determining work or family roles, and singledom has increased in perceived value, all while psychology continues to shame these now-typical behaviors as being "sick."

Sex Outside the Lines will help instill confidence in an authentic sexuality in our sexually dysfunctional culture by dismantling the outdated concepts of "natural" and "normative."

For example, queer ecology, with its acknowledgment of animals with same-sex partnerships, trans- and intersex identities, polyamory, single parenting, and universal non-normative behaviors, devours and annihilates any concept of a "natural" way to be sexual. Compared to humanity, nature is both liberated and radical in its ideas of what is normal.

When you learn to have sex without limits, you will open yourself up to more options for sexuality and relationships, the ability to challenge current sexual categories, and finally, a liberation of your sexuality from shame. Authentic sexuality means that "normal" is *not* the goal.

CHAPTER 1.

LIBERATE SEX AND GET NAKED

WHEN IT COMES TO SEX, "NORMAL" IS NOT THE GOAL

In sex and relationships, "normal" is a dirty word. It's psychologically offensive and needs to be removed from our sexual lexicon. The definition of "normal" is formed by Western, white, male, heterosexual, able-bodied, upper-class individuals, and it works to enforce heterosexuality, monogamy, intercourse-based sexuality, pro-family and pro-marriage views, and neurotypical, cisgendered bodies. If you don't fit into all of those categories, you're not normal, and there's nothing you can do about it.

"Normal" sex stereotypically involves "heterosexual, married, monogamous, procreative, non-commercial, in pairs, in a relationship, same generation, in private, no pornography, bodies only, vanilla" (Rubin, 1984, p. 280). "Normal" is nothing short of a derogatory term, and it should be avoided at all costs within sexuality and relationships (and elsewhere in life too!). The concept of "normalcy" is designed to subjugate people who have the "wrong" bodies (or sexual interests, or body types, etc.). It is psychologically offensive and needs to be extinguished, no longer used as a reference point to determine mental or sexual-relational health. "Normal" is the death of highly pleasurable sex. The "normal" path is very narrow and built from a heteronormative, pro-family, intercourse-centric perspective. Labels such as "slut," "sex addict," and "low sexual desire" are used to police sexual behavior that doesn't fit perfectly into what those in charge believe the vast majority of people are doing. These labels are born out of our culture's sex-negative attitude and must be stopped.

A common definition for unacceptable sex is "sex through distance, through pain, sex with things, with too few or too many Others, with wrong body parts, within similar gender groups." But the limits on what is "normal" by that definition disallow for the sexualities of those who are or have "disabilities, obese, anorexic, depressed, cognitively or affectively disabled… homeless, impoverished" (L. Davis, 2013b, p. 4). The concepts of "normal" and "healthy" sex always align themselves with normative trajectories of both sexual-relational development and "appropriate" ways of being. "In contemporary Western cultures, one [who deviates from this path] is not merely a 'pervert'; one can also be diagnosed with sexual compulsivity, gender [dysphoria], masochism, sadism, obsessive-compulsive disorder, paraphilia, or addiction—or, in common parlance, one is unhealthy, unstable, oversexed, sick" (McRuer & Mollow, 2012, p. 26).

Your marker of good health should never be to have "normal" sex. "Normal" is *not* the goal. "Normal" is a statistical average that ignores the diversity in life and sex and attempts to neutralize exceptionality and creativity. Norms are the status quo. They dilute the most arousing parts of our sexuality and sexual behavior and related arousal. People are routinely convinced that they are emotionally unbalanced because of their sexuality and relational styles when *all* parts of your sexuality and arousal patterns are acceptable and should carry *no* shame. The more we allow ourselves to engage with everything that arouses us, the more our sense of sexual shame and the related isolation diminishes.

"Normal" is held in place by privilege. The gay marriage debate exemplifies the flawed idea of assimilation or "extending the privilege" as a solution for an oppression caused by the institutionalizing of sex and relationships. A completely open system for marriage is a basic human right, but merely allowing more people to marry still maintains a system of dominance and exclusivity and does not remove privilege for certain types of people and forms of relationships. Instead, the dominant ideology, system, or institution needs to be eliminated altogether. Its maintenance means that other minority individuals are still left disenfranchised and faced with discrimination. Extending the scope of what encompasses "normal" and "healthy" is not the solution. Sexual elitism—that is, thinking that your sexuality is the only right or just sexuality while oppressing the sexualities of others—is simply prejudice dressed up in another form.

HOW OUR CULTURE DEBASES SEX

The goal of being sexually "healthy" is one of living and thinking in a sex-positive way. Being sex-positive means not demeaning or pathologizing anyone's sexual choices, interests, or expressions. It means not placing monogamy or marriage above open or casual relationships, or saying that kinky sex is better or more honest than vanilla sex. Sexual activism, sexual health, and sex positivity are about a perspective and a lifestyle of not perpetuating or creating "norms" or policing the borders of what is "acceptable" when sex is consensual, non-damaging, and pleasurable.

Being sex-positive means you're open, flexible, and nonjudgmental about your sexual preferences. It also means allowing your partners to feel the same way without shaming them. I work with far too many cases where couples enter therapy deeming a certain preference problematic. "It's not normal" is a common lament. Often people don't encourage sexual creativity in their partners, instead looking to notions of "normal" to define boundaries. Attempts to "marry" and "monogamize" a sexual partner stem from the anxious drive to regulate anxiety, not from what's emotionally healthy.

Sexual integrity means living in ways that honor what arouses you and are consistent with your own chosen value system, not a system you may have inherited from mainstream culture, psychology, religion, law, or the media. These "outliers" or rebels, those having sex outside the lines designated by mainstream culture and its "experts," exemplify the template for sustainable and healthy sexuality. Exhibiting a different sexual development trajectory doesn't mean you're troubled. Relational sex and partnered sex have been touted as dominant cultural-psychological ideals, but this doesn't make them healthy, or appropriate for everyone. There is a psychological brilliance in those who do not internalize cultural norms and instead create their own paths of growth.

Far too many people accept the sexual-relational myths of mainstream society as soon as they begin dating and becoming sexual, without questioning the validity of or need for any of them. This closed system lacks intelligent critical analysis and keeps people trapped and under the control of our dominant sex-negative culture.

Sexual "appropriateness" and socially sanctioned boundaries of what can be spoken of, questioned, and enacted are ruled by the social process of conformity. We have to culturally determine what is considered sexual, which body parts are found sexual, and what their social meanings are. As innate as sexuality seems, our socialization and social constructions overpower our biology and evolutionary drives. Demarcating only genitals as being sexual, for example, ignores the vast geography of our bodies, and consequently limits sex. Our entire bodies are sexual and hold the possibility of pleasure.

Framing sex as private only limits public sexual expression and relational health. All parts of our bodies are both sexual and nonsexual simultaneously and consistently. Defining sexual language and anatomical verbiage as inappropriate shuts down communication and builds needless shame, while also distancing individuals from their bodies. The sexual realm is deeply impacted by "languaging;" words deeply shape how people experience their own sexuality, and the sexualities of others. Those who are afraid of sex use anti-sex language and silence pro-sex expression, damaging others because they are damaged themselves.

"Eating and sex are both bodily functions. They're both satisfying and gratifying, they both feed the soul, but suddenly, because of our conditioning, one has this sociable aspect to it and the other has to be kept quiet, ignored, and hidden in the corner" (Thomas, 1996, p. 57). We will know we have moved beyond a childish approach to sexuality when we no longer label certain words as sexually inappropriate. Verbal policing leads to the demise of sexual confidence and intelligence. Erotic intelligence involves the ability to confidently speak about sexuality both openly and honestly. Immature sexuality uses euphemisms or avoidance, or designates arousal-specific dialogue as private. Having low erotic intelligence means hiding your sexuality socially and publicly.

The dehumanizing concept of sexual privilege—where some sexual behaviors are arbitrarily deemed better or healthier than others—reduces the diversity and possibility of long-term partnered sex and sexual happiness. What we as a society label sexually "normal" kills arousal and is the trigger for sexual and relational boredom.

Deviance and Stigma

We as a culture treat sexual behaviors that are not within the "norm" as sexually deviant. Deviance, as a label, is about socially created expectations and not about an individual's psychology. In terms of sexuality, deviance is the sign of sexual confidence and health. What I call "sexual-relational rebels" are evolved individuals fighting against a culture that limits sexual freedom, health, and expression. The idea of deviance is not something intrinsic to an individual; deviance and abnormality are socially defined by groups and individuals in power. Deviance should be considered a badge of individuation and honor.

Another way society controls how we think about sex is by stigmatizing it. Stigma is created when we shame certain behaviors and thoughts. Often this is an attempt by those too afraid to acknowledge what they are aroused by or fear in others. A common form of sexual stigmatizing is "slut shaming," or using a person's sexual or relational past to demean them. This is a form of sexual projection where the "slut" is made to bear the anxiety that the accuser cannot contain. The issue is not the sexual preference or sexuality of an individual, but instead the "inequalities, negative attitudes, misrepresentations, and institutional practices that result from the process of stigmatization" (Garland-Thomson, 1997, p. 32). Our anti-nudity and public-sex laws are products of this same misguided thinking: "I will control your behavior because I cannot control my anxieties and emotions."

Here's the problem. Too often, neurological and biological diversity are seen as flaws and deformities to be normalized, corrected, and "fixed." This form of modern-day eugenics is an attempt to regulate socially defined "abnormal" bodies as inferior and unworthy of existence. There is a "broad array of cultural norms that privilege an illusory ideal mind and body at the expense of actual bodies of all shapes and sizes" (Wilkerson, 2011, p. 197). This applies to sex and relationships where psychiatry and psychology use the same erroneous medical model to correct alternative ways of being and relating. Alternative bodies and brains are no more disabled or abnormal than alternative sexualities, identities, or relational styles. The existence of "disability" as an identifier or category strengthens the medical and psychological industries' control and abuse of non-normative and alternative bodies and minds. The new cultures and terms like "neuroqueer" and "neuroatypical"—terms from autistics and other psychologically stigmatized groups who are now challenging the concept that they are "disordered"—allow what was once a designated minority community to declassify themselves from the social stigma that disempowered and dehumanized them. Diagnoses consistently change due to current social mores and politics, demonstrating their flimsy and arbitrary nature.

Calling something deviant or attaching a stigma to it leads to the diagnosing of alternative and different psychologies as unhealthy or broken. Most sexual diagnosing shames people interested in sexual-relational creativity and behavioral nonconformity. Arousing and healthy sexuality requires the very behaviors and fantasies that our sex-phobic institutions and culture want to annihilate. It's ironic that in a society that eagerly devours sexual self-help articles and books and attends sex therapy, novelty and diversity are routinely dismissed or attached with negative stigmas.

Social control and conformity are strengthened by individual acts, like referring to certain sexual behaviors as "normal" or labeling and shaming others as "abnormal." Sexual preferences need to be rescued from oppressive labels like "fetish" or "paraphilia." We all have the right to our chosen sexuality, as sex is the right to selfhood. Shaming sex shames the self. Truly "healthy" sex is a personal choice divorced from inherited morals and the values of the current culture, including "experts" and their laws, which can instead enforce "a powerful taboo against direct representation of erotic activities" (Rubin, 1984, p. 289).

While the Constitution doesn't mention sexual freedom, sexual rights, or sexual protection, the ACLU is an example of a group that works tirelessly to defend sexual rights and expression. Sexual health requires both open dialogue and freedom of expression, and this will, in our sexphobic culture, make many people anxious. But we cannot allow sex to be censored and silenced simply because it scares some people. Emotional comfort is the death of sexuality and arousal. And so the battle continues. Obscenity laws work to undermine all this, as they allow for arbitrary sex regulation, which endangers free expression. Unfettered discussion about sex still suffers second-class status.

What's needed is a form of erotic justice where both sexual shaming and privileging are prohibited. Erotic justice carries with it the goal of not having external regulators controlling our bodies and our sexuality. Examples of how our personal sexual power has been stolen include sex for profit being illegal, Plan B not being available over the counter, decisions about whom and how we marry being made for us, and sex magically being made okay and healthy just by signing a marital contract.

The most important psychosexual component of erotic justice is living in a shame-free environment. "People who were brought up feeling guilty and ashamed of their sexuality do not feel positive about themselves and cannot relate comfortably to people in other areas as well" (Ehrenberg & Ehrenberg, 1988, p. 14). The existence of any shame limits an individual's freedom of thought and choice. Identifying only with predetermined identities and behaviors leaves out myriad alternative sexual and relational selves, including behaviors, desires, and fantasies. This distances the self from itself, the self from the other, and the self from the world.

Sexuality is a socially created construct, and as such it is sensitive and subject to all current cultural dilemmas and struggles. We are born with a sexual response system and drive, but understanding our sexuality (knowledge, theories, and presentations of sex and relationships) and the idea that we are responding to sex "naturally" or "neutrally" is far from reality. We are all socialized as to how we should view sexuality and relationships, and we are provided culturally sanctioned models for how to have sex in a "healthy" way. Ironically, these models are constantly replaced, with new paradigms of "normal" eclipsing past ones.

Sex Workers Will Save Us

A culture's social value system of morality generally communicates more about that society than it does about those whom that society has labeled "deviant." Foucault saw the body as an "inscribed surface of events, traced by language." This speaks to how our bodies and related sexuality are created by history and culture, and are infused with representational dynamics due to the languaging we use to invent and manage ourselves. It's an internalized colonization of the external references of functionality.

"Sexuality" and "body" are both cultural creations that are managed and sustained by our policing of their boundaries. We use terms such as "appropriate," "harassment," and "deviant" to define what is "healthy" and what is a "disorder" or a "crime." These words are merely constructs, lacking consistent and clear definitions. What is determined to be "sexually deviant" differs depending on the culture and time period. Where should one look to explore what is "healthy" or "appropriate" sexually or relationally?

Sex-shaming labels like "porn," "stripper," "sex addict," and "prostitute" are signs of our society's continued sexphobia. Negatively framing these forms of sexuality demonstrates our culturally anxious and fear-based relationship with sex. A sexually healthy culture would integrate and support these diverse and highly arousing concepts. These outlets are a counterbalance to our sex-negative world. We will know we have evolved sexually when these forms are no longer pathologized and shamed. Pornography, sex work, and labels such as "sex addiction" expose our culture to itself, showing us "a detailed blueprint of the culture's anxieties" (Kipnis, 2007, p. 162). Erotica, sex work, and higher sex drives are not forms of illness or deviance. They are all healthy and very common aspects of human sexuality.

Within sex we often prioritize and overemphasize intimacy, as though this experience legitimizes a sexual encounter. But sex can also be recreational, profitable, and pursue various other goals. Intimacy may not be the sought-after goal, and yet intimacy is still possible, if desired, via sex work, massage, and one-time-only anonymous sex. The slandering of "objectified" sex is misguided, as even marital sex full of love and commitment can often be objectified. There is nothing necessarily dehumanizing or unhealthy about an experience wherein one partner focuses on his or her own arousal while ignoring his or her partner's experience.

The Internet provides the largest and most comprehensive catalogue of sexuality available, thereby demonstrating the vast diversity that is "sexuality" in all its various forms. Surprisingly—or not—what isn't generally sought after online is marital, missionary-style, slow, affectionate sex with vaginal penetration. The most frequent porn search keywords are not what are considered "normal." They fall under more diverse categories, such as MILFs, youth, cheating wives, and transsexuals, thereby demonstrating that creative and diverse sexuality actually *is* normal.

What psychology and culture deem "abnormal" is actually highly normal. What the majority may call "deviant" is typical and common. Things that have been stigmatized are in fact healthy and integral parts of arousing sexuality. "Majority" ideology and its "eugenic gaze" does not equate to or make something psychologically, developmentally, or morally healthy.

We need liberation from normative sexual discourse in order to save ourselves from cultural sexual-relational shame. The modeling of obedience to these norms strengthens their power, whereas challenging norms and definitions leads to sexual freedom.

We *All* Must Come Out

Let's explore some anti–sexual freedom double standards. One can watch football or sitcoms on television all day, but to watch erotica (or what many call "porn") regularly is considered addictive behavior. Many will use a film or book to "check out" for relaxing self-care but are shamed if they do the same with masturbation. Travel for sightseeing is great, but to travel for sexual variety isn't supported. Clubs and spaces for drinking and dancing are sanctioned and legal, but clubs for finding sex partners are not. Sex workers and strip clubs are forbidden in the same locations where one can easily find Victoria's Secret storefronts and billboards, which are selling the same kind of eroticism.

The idea that one must distance oneself from or hide one's sexual identities is impossible. Sexuality is everywhere and in everything. It's in how we dress, what we say, and how we say it. Far more harm is caused by sexual repression than by sexual expression.

Society's norms constantly force us to ask ourselves: Is it okay to publicly acknowledge that I'm a sexual being? Should I take others' sexual anxieties into account? For example, what if a client of mine saw me on a sex-seeking app? Would I be deemed less competent? Based on what? The idea that I engage in what's considered a form of societally reckless sex? This compromise should not have to be made, as healthy sexuality is based on sexual freedom and full expression.

Sex is healthy so it should never be hidden or bastardized. When one ignores one's various sexual parts, "the individual ceases to be himself; he adopts entirely the kind of personality offered to him by cultural patterns; he therefore becomes exactly as all others are and as they expect him to be" (Fromm, 1969, p. 184). Those who can embody and live out their sexuality on their own terms are far healthier and more evolved than those who disown their sexuality. I encourage individuals to openly and proudly discuss *all* parts of themselves, especially their sexuality. No one should have to assimilate into a life where sex is solely a means to express love or for procreation.

To fully express your sexuality does not endanger anyone, damage anyone, or make spaces unsafe. In fact, this sort of sexual confidence and respect is the antidote to sexual violence. Sexual health is sexual freedom and not sexual policing and regulation.

Deviation Is the Norm

Our society's vision of what is sexually healthy is taken from a limited menu of cultural options. As we expand our sexual possibilities, what's deemed acceptable will change and true sexual-relational freedom will follow. Sexual behavior is not driven by a reproductive urge, just as variation is not always about adaptation or survival. Diversity reigns supreme as an asset. Sadly, the misunderstood concept of "natural" is almost always used to stigmatize and shame.

Biodiversity and its sexual versatility are what "strengthen the ability of a species to respond 'creatively' to a highly changeable and 'unpredictable' world" (Bagemihl, 1999, p. 251). Nature is a constellation of diverse behaviors and systems. The idea that sexual "abnormality" or "deviance" is inferior or disordered is on its way to extinction. You have the right to be different sexually, relationally, and with your chosen identity. For overall sexual-relational health, normal is *not* the goal.

CHAPTER 2.

WHY WE'RE SCARED OF SEX

If you're a person with sex and relationship interests outside the norm, you've probably been made to feel like you're sick or a freak at some point in your life. Don't worry—you're not the sick one, your culture is.

The current practice for dealing with people who identify as sexually different is to diagnose them as mentally ill, or to try to find a reason in their past that might have caused them to become "deviant" (a catch-all phrase that simply means "not normal"). This idea that somehow it's your fault that you have certain sexual proclivities leads to victim-blaming, as individuals are held responsible for not meeting cultural standards. But institutions such as marriage, monogamy, intimacy, and commitment (all cultural norms) are difficult. The high rates of divorce, singledom, single parenting, and cheating demonstrate a real struggle of the majority to successfully carry out these concepts and ideals in their everyday lives. The sheer number of failures—a steady 45–70 percent for both divorce and cheating—means that the blame lies with the construct and not every individual, since more people fail than succeed.

The outcome of this unachievable societal goal is that individuals see themselves as failures when they cheat (or are cheated on) or when they divorce. This does not imply that we need more marital therapy or more self-help books; our problem is much bigger and requires a much more radical solution. We need to seriously question why we feel the need to push others into relationships or sexual expectations that don't work for them. Why do we care what anyone else does in their bedroom?

The current way we run marriage and monogamy are not always pro-individual, and in fact can often work against a person's relational best interest. The full and complicated history of marriage is beyond the scope of this book, but research shows that equating marriage and monogamy with love is relatively historically recent. There has never been a time in history when extra-relational (meaning outside a primary partnership) sex did not occur and when marriage was a complete success for everyone involved. It's time to distance ourselves from broken concepts like marriage and monogamy, and focus on new, healthy visions for sex and relationships.

Humans are imprisoned within current ideals, "which have become so intimately a part of them that they no longer experience these systems as a series of confinements by embracing them as the very structure of being human" (Bernauer, 1988, p. 45). Instead of confining and shaming one another because we can't live up to the norms, ideologies, and institutions (religion, psychology, family, medicine, and law) of our culture, we should be providing individuals with support. Individuals cannot expect to have healthy sex and relationships within a culture that espouses our current ideologies.

My clinical work and experience highlights the misdirected shaming and blaming that occurs. Most marital conflict I see stems from the current social template for what marriage and commitment should look like. Conflicts and struggles within a structure are a sign of individual health. It takes a rare temperament and psychology to be able to tolerate this arrangement with no issues. The idea of asking a person to choose a partner for life, often at an emotionally young age and regardless of who they may both become later in life, is ridiculous and far from needed. My clients who struggle with this and see it as unhealthy are both correct and very healthy, and more importantly, they are demonstrating a lot of integrity and honesty. A fear of relationships and intimacy is not a disorder but a rational response to our current hostage-like, anti-relational, and unhealthy anti-sex templates for relationships and sex. Our culture is obsessed with a solo and separate self model for relationships, and this hides the fact that relationships are about mergers and codependence. Current theory sees health and maturity as individualism and "standing on your own," ignoring that growth only occurs within and through relationships.

My clinical work has shown that we are all many different people, at many different times, in many different relationships. Our needs shift frequently due to social climate, historical moment, and our multiple and various relationships; our romantic relational commitments should certainly have a similar fluidity. Inconsistency, changing needs, and shifting desires are all signs of functionality. Our cultural templates for healthy sex and relationships do not honor these healthy traits, and, in fact, actively work against them.

Our culture lacks a serious critical lens with which to examine and recreate social norms and institutions. We place dominant rituals upon minorities and outliers, and then punish them for their failures. Our labels and definitions of healthy versus unhealthy sex are all symptoms of our current cultural climate and politics. Homosexuality and masturbation were both once considered sins and disorders. There will be a time in our future when we look back at what we now shame sexually and shake our heads at its stupidity. We do not need more assimilation and immersion; we need a radical reorganization to eliminate many of our social rituals and sexual-relational expectations.

People failing to live up to anxiety-based grand relational-sexual narratives are not bad people. Stop looking into yourself for reasons for failure, and instead look externally at the vision you are carrying as your goal. The misdirected cries of "once a cheater always a cheater" or, within psychology, "cheaters have intimacy disorders or sex addictions" are shaming attempts to maintain a broken structure by blaming the individual who is healthy enough to not be successful. If culture and psychology supported more diverse options for relational configurations, and law and religion sanctioned and legitimized them, we would have healthier relationships. Psychology, law, and religion should be congruent with our current wants and needs rather than forcing us to meet their archaic limited aspirations. These relationally and sexually antiquated modes of policing that support only procreative, heterosexual, two-person, gender-appropriate norms needs to be dismantled.

What's Wrong in the Therapist's Office

I see many couples whose problems stem from being forced into a two-person, monogamous relationship. Unfortunately, the most popular marriage-counseling practices are all based in a model that reveres the two-person, monogamous relationship as the only option considered and presented. This is problematic because there is no room to accommodate non-monogamous, multi-personed, or non-hetero individuals, even going so far as to demonize or pathologize those people. Even for a married hetero couple, these models work to propel people into problematic relationships. Instead of recognizing some of the possible issues inherent in a two-person system and providing other relational options—such as not living together, avoiding marriage, or challenging the limits of sex lives or monogamy—therapists hold the couple in this "one size *must* fit all" configuration and shame them for any failures, even imagined ones. The originators of these models have not evolved their theories to meet the needs and desires of modern identity concepts and relational configurations. A radical shift is needed to work with the needs of all couples seeking help.

If these current models were competent and proficient, the rates of relational dissatisfaction, divorce, and singledom would not be as high as they are. We need to recognize that there are other healthy ways of relating and attempt to move toward them. These traditional models continue to force individuals into ideologies that are not healthy, keeping people trapped in situations that make them unhappy. None of these theorists ever suggest anything more than "work harder on what's already not working." I blame a lack of creativity, critical examination, and analysis within the therapeutic community for the continued use of these models.

The Dangers of Science

Many of our so-called "scientific" paradigms and concepts about sex and relationships have been misinterpreted and are often incorrect, yet they are ubiquitous in popular books and theories about sexuality and gendered behavior. These ideas ignore the impact of socialization, intrapersonal psychology, and the fluidity of self. The most damaging to sexuality and relationship are Darwinian and evolutionary concepts about gender, courting, and mating. Due to these models, we are trained to carry perspectives on sex that are shaming, nonproductive, and just plain incorrect. The concepts of sexual essentialism, erotophobia, hierarchy of sex, evolutionary theories, ideals of nature, and sex addiction all form the constellation that problematizes sex.

Let's explore these ideas a little more fully.

1. Sexual Essentialism

This is the idea that every person has an essential, basic, or core sexuality—which is simply wrong. Sexuality is highly mutable and always under development. We are not inherently geared toward any basic form of sex, as there can be nothing "inherent" about sex. The sheer diversity of sex and sexual interests should make it obvious that there is no such thing as consistent sexuality. The external institutional forces of culture, relationships, and politics interject their influences continually. Sex is not naturally or necessarily even directed toward another person. Solo sexuality (masturbation), asexuality, erotica (pornography), and sexuality with objects (fetishes) are all appropriate sexual desires and manifestations.

2. Erotophobia

"Erotophobia may be defined as the terrifying, irrational reaction to the erotic which makes individuals and society vulnerable to psychological and social control" (Patton, 1985, p. 103). Diagnosing someone with erotophobia is an attempt to reduce, remove, or ignore the presence of his or her sexuality due to fear or disapproval. The manifestation of erotophobia takes several forms.

1. **Marginalization**—This is when categories of sexual identity, sexual behaviors, and relational configurations are ostracized. When this happens, an individual's entire self is reduced to his or her behavioral choices, and he or she is treated poorly due to this alternative sexual-relational decision-making.
2. **Colonization**—The dominant culture determines what is correct and allowed, and then imposes it upon others. No examples of Other cultures are used in education or the media except by way of warning, rehabilitation, or policing.
3. **Pathologization**—Through this process, categories of individuals and behaviors have their diversity removed,

and are not represented as viable or allowed (medically or legally). Psychology uses anti-sex and anti-diversity diagnoses (sex addiction, love addiction, paraphilias). Legal, medical, and psychological practitioners assume that any sexual-relational choices that fall outside the lines are unhealthy or wrong.

4. **Asexualization**—This is when an individual is assumed to not have a sexuality, and is treated as unattractive or nonsexual. This typically occurs with the disabled, the elderly, adolescents, and those who are neuroatypical and behaviorally creative or diverse (aka mentally ill).

The problem with attempting to marginalize, colonize, pathologize, and asexualize behaviors of others is that these attempts do not remove the "problematic" sex, but instead run it underground and force it to only be expressed in secretive, shame-based ways. The regulation of sex is antisocial and weakens relational and social bonds. Erotophobia turns individuals against themselves and creates distance between consorts, because avoidance of sexuality means avoidance and hiding of the self.

3. Hierarchy of Sex

A hierarchy of sex exists where some forms are prioritized or seen as healthier, better, or more appropriate. This scale, in our society, is based on nothing more than the prioritizing of intercourse-based sexuality. There is no basis by which to determine whether one sexual desire is healthier or better than another. Sex has no true inherent goal other than the one we contextually and historically give it, so its meaning is always subjective and personal. Therefore sexual health is subjective and should be determined by each individual's relational and political ideals.

4. Evolutionary Theory and Privileging of Procreation

Evolutionary theory and sexual-selection theory both disregard and ignore sexuality that exists outside of different-gendered, pair-bonding, procreative sex. Animals and humans all have sex for non-procreative reasons and in non-intercourse-based ways, often with birth control methods, just for pleasure, bonding, and connection. Many animals have friendships mediated by sex and use sexual behavior to socialize. Bonobos and Japanese macaques, for example, both in same-sex and opposite-sex formations, use both oral and anal sex to make friendships, regulate aggression and conflicts, and often just for fun. Studies prove time and again that animals have sex that is not exclusively for procreation and the perpetuation of genes. The idea of sex existing solely for gene dispersion and procreation is limited, ignoring the realities of both human and animal sexual behaviors. This concept is problematic because a lot of research uses it as a reference point for medical, psychological, sexological, and sociological theory and praxis.

5. Ideals of Nature

The concept of what is "natural" has been used to abuse and oppress alternative relational styles and sexuality throughout history. There needs to be an honest acknowledgment of "the vast range of same-sex acts, same-sex child-rearing pairs, intersex animals, multiple 'genders,' 'transvestism,' and transsexuality existing throughout the more-than-human world" (Alaimo, 2010, p. 52).

The idea of "natural" is referenced to challenge the validity of behaviors that make some uncomfortable. The flaw in this reasoning is that nature is very diverse and contains manifestations that are congruent with all human relationships. Plants, animals, and fungi show a wealth of diversity and are not single-sexed, pair-bonded, monogamous, single-gendered beings. Yet they are perceived to be, and the paradigm of doing something "against nature" is utilized to define unacceptable behavior. "Single parenting, or indeed no parental investment at all, is the *norm* in the nonhuman living world...yet, in human cultures, single parenting is seen as the antithesis of the natural order of things..." (Hird, 2008a, p. 234). Animals have sex for pleasure only, they masturbate, they use varying methods of birth control (vaginal plugs, abortion through ingestion, ejection of sperm), they modify objects for vaginal and anal insertion, and they have sex between species (sexual behavior between plants and insects is commonplace) (Hird, 2008a, p. 235; Alaimo, 2010, p. 61).

Attempting to separate nature (biology) from culture (socialization) is useless. Therefore, whatever an individual does behaviorally is both natural and biologically driven. The sexologist Alfred Kinsey is quoted as saying "the only unnatural sex act is that which you cannot perform."

6. Sex Addiction

One of the largest and most diluted modern forms of sexual hysteria and panic is the sex addiction theory. This Trojan horse has carried within it a lot of sexphobia and confusion. Sex addiction masquerades as a diagnosis that requires treatment and therapy, but it actually damages and vandalizes sexuality. With an eroto-negative gaze, this concept has allowed for the psychology field and those in the media to abuse those forms of relationships and sex that make them anxious or confused. The creation of apostles to this religion—sex-addiction therapists—perpetuates and disseminates this flimsy pseudoscience-based idea. In fact, the universal mental health diagnostic manual (the

DSM V) rejected attempts to have sex addiction included as a legitimate diagnostic issue, meaning that the highest authorities in the field of mental health find it void of universal criteria and laden with far too many political-moral values. Sexuality is an ever-present drive, like hunger, that is always operating within and upon most of us, guiding our behavior and our erotic gaze. This energy and drive cannot be an addiction. Sex can become problematic, but this is because of a lack of adequate sex education and a misunderstanding of what healthy sex looks like. This includes acceptance of an individual's authentic arousal constellation, consisting of everything that turns them on. Commonly, confusion exists around how to get sexual interests met with a partner whom you are no longer attracted to, with a partner who has only limited sexual interests and many sexual walls, or due to lack of awareness that masturbation daily or more often, and with pornography, is common. Sexuality is made problematic when parts of our sexual selves are run underground due to shame, which always forces their manifestation somewhere.

The larger issue with the sex-addiction theory is its attempts to police non-normative sexuality. Its criteria for diagnosing reads like a sex-hating to-do list. The sex-addiction theory rules out all highly stimulating and arousing forms of erotic potential and refers to activities such as paying for sex, sex to self-soothe and reduce stress, sex for entertainment, traveling for sex, frequent masturbation, sex outside a monogamous relationship, and watching others have sex as addictive behavior. A healthy sexual person could practically use the list of behaviors that sex-addiction therapists discourage as a guide to keeping sex varied and fun.

Erotic Plasticity

Most sexual-relational "problems" are *not* the behavior itself, but our culture's treatment of it. We take our pseudoscientific criteria from the "human sciences" (psychiatry, medicine, and psychology), and if an individual doesn't fit into the proper categories, we classify him or her as "sick" or "perverted." The sociology of perception demonstrates how we all perceive sensory information differently within culture and history. As such, we are socialized to look for specific data that supports our cultural lens and perceptions, and to exclude that which is not relevant to our socially trained theories on sex, relationships, and bodies. We collectively have a specific "sexual-relational vision" that "gives rise to perceptual patterns that are neither individual nor universally human. Rather, these patterns are the result of 'optical socialization'" (A. Friedman, 2013, p. 17). Variations and non-norms are ignored, excluded, or made irrelevant. Our "perceptions" (which are actually culturally coded opinions and beliefs) are a part of our social construction of reality.

Expectation influences perception with processes such as confirmation bias and selective attention, which drive us to ignore or discount information that does not support our expectations. "We are 'perceptually readied' to seek out and register those details that reflect our collective expectations… Social salience can at times override empirical salience, leading us to attend to perceptually subtle but socially important information" (A. Friedman, 2013, p. 23). Friedman discusses "sexpectations" as the perceptual readiness to look for gendered cues, but I would extend this to include all diverse sexual-relational-pectations. Our visual and mental search goes further than just filtering others through a lens of gender and body cues, but also includes a schema for what's "right" or "wrong."

Culture, psychology, media, morals, and values can all have a powerful intellectual impact on our cognitive desires, but thankfully, they still have very little control over our psychological and biological drives. The current norms and diagnoses within psychology and psychiatry speak to our culture and the expectations it places upon people. This says far less about the individuals who are diagnosed, as individuals act out cultural and social struggles. Instead, these diagnoses highlight those cultural struggles, as well as "the drive of powerful groups to dominate and purify space" (Johnston & Longhurst, 2010, p. 28). Institutions can shame, pathologize, and normalize certain sexual-relational styles, but this doesn't extinguish our more authentic internal interest, arousal, or drive to have the sex we want, the way we want. Society can normalize monogamous, partnered, committed relational sex, but that will not fend off habituation, boredom, or a need for diversity and liberation from sexual-relational oppression. Our role models (parents, therapists, public figures) lived in a different sexual era, but, more importantly, they most likely never questioned the types of sex, relationships, and sexual standards they maintained. A healthy sexual-relational cultural milieu is one in which multiple configurations and styles are offered and supported as healthy, normal, and functional, versus our current one-option-only culture. We must stop blaming individuals for failure when it is actually the models and expectations that are the problem.

ADULT SEX IS VANDALIZED SEX

Our conceptualization of "mature" and "adult" sexuality is actually the result of a vandalized sexuality and is cultural sexual abuse. It's a repressed and bruised model that stems from cultural attacks, shaming, and fear. Our social constructions of religion, science, and medicine have permanently derailed what could be a "natural" sexuality and put an enduring blemish upon its development, so much so that we cannot untangle its full damage. This cultural sexual abuse shapes our sexual identity and our relationship to our sexuality. This is why sexual health is sexual freedom.

You are free when you can have the sex you want without guilt, shame, labels, or a diagnosis of a mental illness. Much of the sexual-relational behaviors we label as "sex addiction"—such as cheating and objectification—are simply sexuality freed from social, political, and institutional constraints. They demonstrate what our basic sex drive and sexual nature in its purest form could look like, instead of our current one that exists within the context of our social fear, anxieties, and boundaries.

The evolutionary model of sex, which states that sexual activity must only serve the need of species survival, is flawed. It normalizes and prioritizes heterosexual and reproductive sexual behaviors to the exclusion of all else. It ignores the diversity of true sexuality in both humans and animals. It causes other sexual behaviors to be treated as a commentary on and illumination of one's character. The kind of sex we have shouldn't matter to anyone outside of our bedroom; we all deserve to be treated as more than the sum of our sexually chosen behaviors and desires. The reduction of an individual solely to his sexuality is a denial of each person's complexity and diversity.

MODELS OF SEX

Our culture conceptualizes sex as something to give away, to keep, to protect, to examine, or to control. These various cultural and social models have consequences for individuals and the way we perceive sex and ourselves. Our culture creates and maintains these models and therefore holds responsibility for their outcomes and consequences. Individuals internalize the following discourses about sex:

1. **Virginity Model**—This model sees sex as a non-renewable resource, with the first time one is sexual as the most prized, and a lessened value thereafter. This

prioritization of purity attempts to determine one's worth and value as based on having sex.

2. **Character Model**—This model utilizes sex to determine one's integrity. What, when, with whom, and how you are sexual is used to determine if you are a "good" person.
3. **Capitalist Model**—This model sees sex as property, something that is under ownership of your partner. Sex is framed as what you do within a relationship and is therefore limited by the boundaries and eroticism of your partner.
4. **Performance Model**—This anatomy- and physiology-based model believes that genitals should only work in a certain specific way, that there is only one right way for arousal, orgasms, bodies, and erections to function.
5. **Shame Model**—This model expects individuals to hide that they are sexual, allowing no overt or open public sexual dialogue or recognition. It does not support the use of erotic capital, where one confidently leads with and utilizes their sexuality for gain and advancement. It includes sexphobic words like "whore," "pervert," and "sex addict."

Instead we should aspire to models such as:

1. **Pleasure Model**—This model frames sex as fluid, non-anatomically and non-genitally based, meaning there is no wrong way to do it and no lens of dysfunction through which to view it. This model has no goal for sexuality but the pursuit of pleasure.
2. **Sexual Health Model**—This model frees individuals by allowing them to have sex for reasons of their choosing, which can include recreation, pleasure, relationship and intimacy building and strengthening, procreation,

profit, and work. It allows for the expression of one's full authentic arousal constellation. Limits on sexuality are avoided and treated as limits on individual freedoms. This model includes the belief that we are not free as long as we cannot decide the conditions under which we are sexual.

CHAPTER 3.

SEX EDUCATION IS DANGEROUS

Sex education in our country today lies, misinforms, and sets people up for a lifetime of sexual problems. Built on avoidance and denial, it's an education in oppression and violence.

Current sex education is often about self-regulation, "interventions on the body" and "programs of disciplinary betterment" (Hook, 2007, p. 23), as opposed to sexual knowledge, health, and confidence. Our general educational system is built on an ethics of training and control. It doesn't challenge the current prejudices around sex, relationship, and identity. What we should be urgently asking about today's sex education is this: Is it liberating people or creating sexual oppression?

Today's sex education generally promotes only the dominant ideas of heterosexuality, monogamy, and marriage. It ignores variation and diversity, bypasses pleasure, and is obsessed with avoidance and abstinence. It privileges "safe" ways of showing sexuality. It discourages honest, open, and direct communication about how broad one's sexuality can be.

Instead of presenting the different choices and identities each individual has to discover on his or her own sexual path, sex education serves to constantly perpetuate the dominant norms of our culture. It's geared toward alleviating parental and institutional anxieties rather than educating individuals about sexual truth and reality. It privileges one perspective while excluding and oppressing all others. What's desperately needed is a reality-based sex education that, rather than focusing on basic anatomy and condom usage, discusses diverse forms of safe sex, full-bodied sexuality, and expanded sexual limits. True learning means challenging one's frame of thought and attitude while also talking about and seeing things that make one uncomfortable. There is no learning or growth without anxiety and crisis. Highly diverse and transgressive sexuality has long been excluded, invisible, and distorted by stereotypes and myths. Every time oppressive sexual discourse is re-taught, sexual abuse occurs.

School is where most adolescents form their relational and sexual identity. It's a place where integration and practice meet, and it's also where education intersects with sex. Most people have sex for the first time while they're in high school, typically starting at age seventeen (Schalet, 2011, p. 3). The adolescent years provide a rich narrative of sexuality formation and active experience. What a person learns during this period can either nourish him or her, or traumatize his or her sexual and relational identity. When educators assume—or are forced to assume by outdated curricula—that their students are all heterosexual, monogamously centered, and sexually traditional, sex education becomes a form of oppression. It avoids challenging young people's frame of thought and attitude, ignoring things and ideas that make those in power uncomfortable.

Sex education focuses on a binary choice: procreation or abstinence. That's not safe sexual education—it's abstinence education. The point of sex education should not be indoctrination into heterosexual, gender-binary, procreative-directed, or pro-marriage ideals. But in our culture today, education, especially around sex, is about assimilation and not freedom or choice. The hidden curriculum is based on biased information and agenda-setting while masquerading as being objective.

Here are the key ways in which our current sex education is most lacking:

1. Teachers are assumed to be "experts," and as such they create the "truths" and narratives students will retain

about their sexuality. Teachers and their curricula are not neutral. This allows for much personal bias and politics.

2. Sex education does not acknowledge that the information being taught is interpretation and not fact. It ignores alternative ideas, interpretations, and truths. It also doesn't explore what impact this kind of exclusion has.

WHERE DID MY SEX GO?

The classroom is a highly sexualized arena. Acknowledging and respecting this ever-present eroticism is necessary, as it allows individuals to learn how to harness and work with their sexuality, whatever form it might take. One of sex education's major flaws is its complete denial and repression of sex until an arbitrary point of acceptability (typically seen as puberty, a committed relationship, or marriage), when it is nervously and chaotically released. Sex education should deal with allowing this kind of expression in ways that are safe and sustainable.

It's taboo to acknowledge how a teacher's sexuality impacts his or her work. Yet a teacher's sexuality is an integral part of learning about erotic capital, as sexuality is always being taught and modeled. In a real-world sex education class, understanding how sexuality interacts with professionalism is a much-needed lesson for teachers and students alike. We attempt to erase sex from public spaces like classrooms, yet a healthy relationship to sex requires an acknowledgment of its constant presence and influence. Healthy educational professionals are aware of this. "We do teach our sexualities. Sexuality is part of who we are, and it does not go away when we enter our classrooms" (Nuñez, 2012, p. 85). Nor should it. The personhood of a teacher is always itself an education, and a teacher's relationship to sexuality should be utilized. Educators have an opportunity to model the message of sex as being integrated: it's always present and always healthy as long as one claims one's sexuality and sexual body with confidence. "Learning about a sex act doesn't toggle the desire switch to 'on' or the body switch to 'go'" (Levine, 2003, p. 8). Learning and knowing does *not* automatically lead to doing.

The comfort of living one's sexuality and gender via clothing, hairstyle, and behaviors is another area where our erotophobic cultural perspective bleeds into pedagogy. Every moment in the classroom is an education. We cannot have a sexually healthy culture or an educational system free from rape and bullying if we disrespect sexuality by striving to maintain distance from it. Learning how to encounter and manage sexuality needs to begin early in real-time classroom situations, not just theoretically via classroom discussion. Covering up all the sexual "sharp edges" so no child bumps into sex helps no one, because it preserves the notion that sex is bad and dangerous. This repression builds up a tension that leads to chaos and confusion.

Children and adolescents need to learn how to approach and navigate all forms of sexuality in order to build their confidence and competence with its management. Denying the ubiquitous nature of sex leaves the learning for the random, uncontrolled occasions when sex is encountered. Individuals cannot be held accountable for appropriately managing skills and behaviors that they have been taught to avoid and fear. Forcing sexuality to be avoided or ignored limits people's comfort with navigating its existence. Consistent policing and amputation of the sexual body serves no one, and it only breeds anxiety with its presence and usage.

MEDIA EDUCATION RUINS SEX

The media is not only the most powerful form of socialization, it's the leading sex educator in America. The media has a monopoly on shaping how our country thinks, speaks, writes, and, in particular, treats sex. It uses stereotypes, distorts reality, and overdramatizes narratives, reinforcing a fundamentally conservative and overly moralistic approach toward sex. This both consciously and subconsciously constructs personal and social attitudes toward sexuality. In a media-driven sex education, morals and sexual health are inextricably linked.

Advertisements, many magazines, and news outlets reinforce problematic narratives and sexist, biased ideologies. Genders are always clearly male or female in advertising, and relationships are always heterosexual, monogamous, and nuclear-family centered. There are no representations of polyamory, transsexuals, open marriages, sex-for-fun-only relationships, or alternative family configurations. All of these alternatives are healthy, reality-based forms of sexual expression and should be celebrated and normalized. Yet they're ignored by advertisers. This sends a strong message about what society considers acceptable. Why can't I see a mixed-race, queer, trans family in a soap commercial?

Many focus on and reinforce common problematic notions of gender and sex. There is no "female" or "male" sexuality to address as much as there is a need to address the physical and superficial differences between women and men. This remedial separation of male and female gender perpetuates the idea of a distance between them and distinct sexualities and psychologies for both, when in fact these don't exist. People of all genders struggle with similar issues sexually, and when their struggles differ, the differences are far more nuanced than merely being based on gender.

Above all this, of course, is social media, now one of the most powerful forms of sexual socialization and education. Ubiquitous and easily accessible, social media (Facebook, Twitter, Instagram, and sex/dating apps like Grindr, Tinder, etc.) build sexual psyches by forming and solidifying people's perceptions about sex, bodies, social values, and norms. What you expose yourself to literally forms your ideals and value system. The images that we consume via social media have a massive influence over our self-esteem and body image. Social media also creates a psychological and social role model to aspire to, as the images we surround ourselves with help form our internal working model of what we consider attractive, acceptable, and "normal."

It's important to explore the psychological and social environments from which we allow our views to be constructed. Social media is how we market ourselves. The pictures we post and the statements we make brand us and show others how we want to be perceived. This occurs both consciously and unconsciously, so much so that you can undermine the way you'd prefer to be publicly perceived by not being aware that you're following or viewing posts and images that do not support the values you admire and aspire to.

What magazines are on your coffee table? What TV shows do you watch? Who do you follow on Instagram? When working with clients, I always explore the Facebook, Twitter, and Instagram accounts they follow, as these outlets make up a large part of our everyday socialization. They become a powerful social authority that dictates norms and expectations. To ignore them is to miss out on a window into a person's social culture and sexual customs.

Used properly, social media platforms can create a nourishing and supportive environment of influence. Used improperly, they can create a toxic, brutalizing atmosphere of detrimental comparison, leading to a debilitating sense of loneliness and an unhealthy desire for unachievable norms. Learning to value or dislike one's body is an acculturation process. You cannot feel good about your body if you are surrounded by images of bodies that do not match your own. We must take responsibility for and make conscious choices about the body and sexual norms we consume and feed to those around us. You will not feel good if your life is full of magazines that reinforce body shame by trafficking in images of bodies that don't mirror your own and help sustain the idea of one acceptable culturally sanctioned body ideal. These images perpetuate body shaming and individual body policing by flaunting one monolithic normative form. Nor will you have a healthy sense of self if you're flooded by tweets containing toxic messages.

We desperately need media and television models that offer sustainable and healthy "imagery to contest and complicate dominant representations of gender, sexuality, race, ethnicity, class, ability, age, body type, and other identity markers...and iconography to expand established sexual norms" (Taormino et al., 2012, p. 9). Any time you use social media, your views on sex, gender, and relationships are being shaped. Be aware of what you allow to influence you. Socialization and normalization often occur outside of your awareness.

The media also negatively impacts our expectations and worldviews of what is "normal." It has a huge influence on what we find sexually arousing and appropriate. The media has a far greater impact on sexual-relational socialization than one's parents do. I'm not aware of any television show, other than my own show *Bad Sex* on Logo TV, that allows individuals to be gender fluid, openly express non-normative sexuality, or be relationally alternative, without shaming any of these creative and brave ways of being.

Due to the power of the media, it's necessary to see "realistic representations of non-normative relationships. When media fail to present realistic portrayals of queer relationships, they are doing a disservice to all of the members of society" (Slagle & Yep, 2007, p. 190). "Queer" in this context doesn't mean explicitly gay or lesbian, but rather a position and way of living that is non-normative. Heterosexuals, homosexuals—indeed, all sexual orientations—can be "queer" if they live outside the lines of hetero- and homonormativity.

LANGUAGE EDUCATES

How sex education is defined, and by whom, often determines a young person's initial sexual identity. Based on the deluge of clients and couples coming into my office, the current models and definitions aren't encouraging long-term sexual-relational health. Sex education needs to be liberating, not indoctrinating. Sex is a learned process born from a complex internal-external drive. It requires options and choices, not more limits.

Countries such as Germany, Sweden, France, and the Netherlands, are pro–sex education in all its forms and diversity, so students learn healthy behaviors and attitudes about sex. This successful approach has led to far less teen pregnancy and far fewer STDs compared to the United States (Schalet, 2011, p. 42). True sex education is non-political and non-theoretical, and it works to transcend traditional and mainstream sexual-health norms.

My work typically involves re-educating patients and helping them free their psyches of the problematic sex education they received from family, friends, psychologists, and teachers. When I'm getting to know a client, I ask them about what kind of education they've had. The answer tells me two important things: 1) What types of things did this kind of education exclude? and 2) Whom did this education oppress?

For example, most high school sex education classes and programs "authorize suppression of a discourse of female sexual desire, promote a discourse of female sexual victimization, and explicitly privilege married heterosexuality over other sexual practices" (M. Fine, 1988, p. 42). Students literally aren't able to imagine a healthy alternative sexuality beyond that which they are taught in school. The very system meant to "educate" about sex instead winds up regulating and limiting the discussion to only those types of sexuality that are considered safe, comfortable, and heteronormative. Education on any topic requires information, elaboration, and exploration. But contemporary sex "education" involves more obfuscation and omission than actual education.

SEXUAL RIGHTS

All humans have sexual rights, regardless of age and orientation. Sexual rights means the right to be sexual, to have a sexuality, and to utilize it as one sees fit. Most sex education, whether it's in the classroom, a church, or the family home, operates from a "refusal to see adolescents as having sexual rights…the right to say yes" (Rasmussen, Rofes, & Talburt, 2004, p. 112). Using sex and the body as sites of resistance against disciplinary practices and attempts to create submissive sexual bodies is a crucial first step in sexual-relational empowerment.

Sexual rights involve using erotic capital, an individual's sexuality and sexual assets, for personal gain. Erotic confidence and sexual sophistication are human strengths that give us a viable advantage in certain situations, just like intelligence and social skills. When sexuality is a healthy, integral part of our lives, there is no need to downplay its presence or ignore its power. Dressing in a way that highlights one's sexuality and eroticism isn't a flaw or a weakness. An integrated, actualized individual does not shun any part of his or her being. In fact, the best way to increase body esteem is to develop pride through exposure. Our culture has deemed certain bodies as exhibiting an attractive sexualized physicality. To express sexual pride and live in one's body fully, regardless of whether you're disabled, skinny, fat, young, old, fit, or not, is to articulate yourself as a sexual being and your body as sexy. Bodily display is the antidote to sexual and body shame. I never shy away from utilizing my eroticism in my personal presentation, style of dress, or interactions. I confidently acknowledge the power of sexuality, and I present myself with this awareness.

That stems in part from knowing what my sexual rights are as a person. What sexual rights is every person entitled to?

1. **Counteracting all misinformation and prejudice.** Start by ignoring everything you've been taught thus far. Prejudicial and sex-negative misinformation is far too ubiquitous in our society. The ways in which you examine and understand sex need to be challenged and then, likely, eliminated. Hold your current opinions and understandings loosely and allow space for new expectations and ideas. How you define sex needs to always be able to be expanded and incorporated into new templates and behaviors.
2. **Elimination of sexual or relational privilege and prejudices.** Growing up, you were most likely taught a belief system that legitimizes certain sexualities and behaviors while declaring others illegitimate. Many sex-ed programs support or educate around "traditional family values." "Traditional" here means two hetero people, one male and one female, having monogamously focused sexual intercourse. "Family" means procreative, marriage-based, and child-focused sex education. The "values" are those held by Western capitalist white males. There are no meaningful or consistent standards upon which to base teaching these beliefs. Dismantle this way of thinking and discard it.
3. **Encouragement of exploration.** Acknowledge and support all sexual alternatives (bastardized clinically as "paraphilias") as healthy options. Not knowing the alternatives leaves many with arousal issues and with lowered sexual desire. Having a wide range of sexual skill and capacities will enhance sexual self-esteem and healthy, sustainable adult sexuality. Try sex that is considered to be "alternative" and utilize sexual

creativity to enhance your sexual life, relationships, and tolerance for others' sexual anxiety.

4. **Elimination of shaming of sexual matters, words, and concepts.** The phrase "sexually inappropriate" turns one person's sexual anxiety into a social boundary or norm to be followed. Using others' sexual anxiety to set your boundaries limits your own sexual freedom. Healthy sexuality means being comfortable discussing sex openly and confidently. Words and concepts such as "virgin," "slut," "sex addict," "fuck buddy," and "one-night stand" devalue sex and damage people's depth, connection, pleasure, intimacy, and capacity for health. Individuals need to be taught clitoral confidence and penis dignity to form a healthy erotic base so as to avoid sexual problems in adulthood.
5. **Acknowledgment and education about webcams and alternative sexualities as safe sex.** Webcam sex and other sexual behaviors without physical contact carry no risk of STDs or unwanted pregnancy because there is no partner, fluid exchange, or bodily contact. Sex via texting, cams, and with objects limits exposure. Kink also teaches people (especially sexual abuse survivors) how to learn boundaries, communication, safety, consent, and liberation, as BDSM requires the use of these communication skills. (Ironically, hetero sex is the most dangerous kind of sex because of the risk of unwanted pregnancy. This risk doesn't exist with sex between same-sexed bodies.)
6. **Fight against genital tyranny.** "Genital tyranny" is sex that sees only the reproductive anatomy as sexual and erogenous. Recognize that the entire body is erogenous. No area should be left un-sexualized or un-pleasured.

EDUCATOR AS WHORE

Historically, the role of the whore was to educate those coming of age about the sexual body. Sex education, like any form of education, requires doing, yet sex is a special case where, culturally, we do not support the idea of practice. Instead we expect marginal, obfuscating discussion to produce good sexual results. The same people who complain of bad sex from their partners send their kids without practice into the sexual world to reenact what they despise and complain about themselves. This is a cycle of sexual abuse.

Learning by doing is how all skill sets are acquired. Virginity sets the stage for disappointing sex due to a lack of practice and experience. Specifically:

- a lack of understanding arousal
- having not learned sexual skills
- body discomfort
- no genital confidence
- no confidence that pleasure is okay
- no sexual communication skills
- no awareness of how broad "safe sex" can be
- no comfort carrying birth control/protection

If there's any good news in this, it's that, as Jen Gilbert states, "school-based sex education may be the least relevant and least persuasive education [youths] receive" (2004, p. 124).

So how do we then create proactive sex-positive education? A healthy sex education would address the following:

> **Sexuality:** Acknowledge that sexuality is a basic part of humanity. It exists not just in the bedroom or between sex partners, but everywhere. Everyone has different levels of sexuality and sex drive, including some who

are asexual and have no sex drive at all, but may masturbate or have interest in affection or sensuality. Everyone is entitled to be sexual. Erasing sexuality is often done to those who are disabled or cognitively or behaviorally atypical ("mentally ill"). This is an attempt to make sex invisible to these groups.

Safe Sex: Redefine this concept to go beyond "condom usage," explaining what it really means: sexual expression that involves no fluid exchange or human penetration. Most safe sex discussion is reduced to only issues of disease transmission, making it no longer about sexuality. The following are all healthy vehicles for safe sex:

- dildos
- vibrators
- toys
- masturbation (both solo and mutual)
- viewing pornography/erotica
- erotic massage
- webcam
- sexting
- exhibitionism
- voyeurism
- stripping
- fantasy play/role playing
- costumes

Sexual Constellation: Explore all the myriad ways individuals can be sexually aroused. This would include (and this list is in no way exhaustive or complete):

- opposite gender
- same gender

- bisexual (both same and opposite sex)
- polysexual, pansexual, and omnisexual (gender irrelevant)
- solo-based (masturbation preference)
- fluid (hetero- and homoflexible)
- asexual (no sexual other)
- fetish (BDSM, group)
- objects (non-human)

Relational Configuration: Learn about some of the many diverse ways individuals build relationships:

- polyamory (multiple relationships at once)
- open (primary but open to sex with others)
- monogamous/closed (primary partner as only sex partner)
- marriage (state-sanctioned commitment)
- swingers (sex with others as a couple)
- solo poly (open style while also not looking for a primary/exclusive partnership)
- mono/poly (one partner is polyamorous and the other is not)

Purpose: Sex has many purposes. There is no right reason for having sex. The desire for sex changes often, even within the same relationship with the same partner. Understand the myriad legitimate purposes of sex, including:

- for pleasure
- for recreation
- for procreation
- to enhance intimacy
- for bonding

- as a coping mechanism
- to relieve boredom
- to enhance love
- to reduce horniness
- to decrease a bad mood
- to reduce stress
- for growth and exploration of self

Anatomy: Our sexual anatomy is our entire body. There are no off-limits body parts for sexuality. Do not limit touching, licking, stroking, or sucking to only the breasts, clitoris, vagina, penis, nipples, or anus. Utilize EVERYTHING!

CHAPTER 4.

THE DAMAGE OF PSYCHOLOGY

Anyone who walks into a bookstore or browses for books online can tell you that, based on the number of self-help books out there, people must be in trouble, especially in the sex and relationship department.

The problem is, most self-help authors and even many mental health practitioners lack adequate training in human sexuality and sex therapy. Would you let a podiatrist perform your heart surgery? Then why are you getting a sex diagnosis from a therapist who has no idea what he's talking about?

"It is rather disturbing that while advertisements in the media are telling consumers to talk with their physicians about sexual concerns, the teaching in medical schools surrounding human sexuality continues to be reduced or eliminated" (Kleinplatz, 2012, p. xxviii). This will be discussed in further in chapter 8, but most so-called sexual dysfunctions are not actual dysfunctions, but the result of sexual miseducation. Erectile dysfunction is commonly promoted on television as a problem, but this is not actually a dysfunction for most; many psychological and social factors, such as not understanding the normal ebbs and flows of penile functioning, are the real cause. This fundamental lack of understanding leads to frequent misdiagnoses, as well as harmful treatments and therapies. Making a perfectly healthy penis the scapegoat for bad sex or relational problems serves no couple's relationship. Viagra and its supporters somehow think the goal should be a robo-penis, hard and ready as needed. Medical practitioners who dispense prescriptions for these pharmaceutical enhancements are operating from a sexphobic, heterocentric, traditionalist viewpoint that shames gender differences and sexual liberation. They use anti-sex models, outdated theories, and sexually questionable treatments to strengthen and perpetuate a pro-hetero-marriage monogamy complex. According to them, if the sex you're having (or want to have) doesn't fit into that box, you're sick, wrong, and abnormal.

Our culture has a deeply biased system of psychological knowledge production, full of internal elitism, with "experts" from a narrow anti-sex pool making all the important value decisions about sexual-relational health. These "experts" perpetuating pathologizing sexual and relational diagnoses are running related treatment centers and writing books and manuals that naïve therapists accept as truth, thereby flooding the psychology field with sex-hating misinformation and lies. Far too many people believe that if a book about an issue exists, or a center that treats it is available, then it must be a true issue. Few are aware that diagnoses like sex and love addiction or codependence are highly contested, and many sexologists and sex therapists (myself included) do not accept them as real. Yet there are books written and treatment centers to take your money to "cure" you of these and other flimsy "issues."

What we really need is a complete overhaul of the way we approach sex therapy. More options must be considered and alternatives must be normalized. There is a real need for "psychology to critically examine itself so that it [can] be a force for transformation rather than for conformity to status quo arrangements" (Watkins & Shulman, 2008, p. 24). Therapy has become a disciplinary institution that works to "correct" and "rehabilitate" behaviors that are socially "deviant" (Hook, 2007, p. 40), rather than healing and helping those who seek it.

Therapists have become moral police instead of healers. Healing is about liberation and freedom, not confinement and monitoring. The work of therapy should be to liberate the mind, not to co-opt it with cultural values and expectations. We should encourage each person to develop his or her own values. Therapy and psychology should strive to liberate people from the detrimental confinements that societal expectations have placed on them.

SEXUAL TERRORISTS

Oppressive diagnoses such as sex addiction and intimacy disorders, and therapies for issues like fetishism and cheating (highly common sexual preferences that should not be treated as disorders) leave clients worse off and shamed by damaging treatments. These false diagnoses *create* suffering and illness, rather than curing or treating them. Mainstream therapists have institutionalized and reified a narrow, hierarchial, prejudicial-anxiety-based view of sex and relationships that leads to negative clinical consequences.

So whom does their work serve? Most sex therapies are forms of social control that police the borders of sexuality. All psychology is power, and most practitioners use the clinical office as a confessional to punish the sexual-relational transgressions that are confessed. These disciplinary actions are supported by the mental health bible, the *DSM*, which itself is flawed and controversial. In addition, psychiatric categories lack cross-cultural universality based on limited research, and are therefore only applicable to middle-class white people in North America, the United Kingdom, and Western Europe (Kleinman, 1988, p. xii). Where is the "science" in using this flawed document as a basis for diagnosis and healing?

Clinical and psychological institutions train from a view that perpetuates the idea that there is a unified and concrete "right" and "wrong" way to behave within relationships and sexuality. But there can be no universally applicable diagnosis of "healthy" or "unhealthy"; each person must determine his or her own methods for arousal and choose desired relational configurations and boundaries based on those methods. Erroneously, many practitioners and "experts" thrust heterosexual, monogamy-focused, two-person-only expectations upon clients in order to determine sexual-relational health. If you aren't interested in a relationship that looks like that, you need to be "fixed."

The concepts of two-partner-only relationships, monogamy as a central boundary, penile-vaginal penetration as the main sexual goal, erection-required sex, and prioritizing of partnered sex over solo sexuality are all colonizing and repressive ideologies. Yet they form the foundational goals for most sexual-relational therapeutic work.

TREATING VERSUS HEALING—MENTAL ILLNESS AS PERFORMANCE

Mental illness is not solely psychological, but is the outcome of a process involving differences from social values, a language of illness labeling, and the consequential reactions and expectations. Therapists need to be aware of what Foucault called the "power of truth construction." He explored how sex is the way to both understand the self and to liberate the self, as sex is the entry point by which "experts" control a person. When therapists, psychologists, and psychiatrists create systems of knowledge, they are also giving themselves the power to make others their subjects, and to use that power to designate patients as criminals, sex addicts, deviants, etc. (D. Epstein & Johnson, 1998, p. 15).

The field of psychological diagnostics creates more illnesses and pulls more people into the medical matrix, rather than freeing individuals from the mental stigmas they've placed on themselves. The social sciences work to build new diagnostic categories and labels, thereby bringing into the world new typologies of people and disordered "patients." This sexual-relational eugenics uses therapy to create a population of "fit" individuals who conform to socially defined health. This "ill versus healthy" idea leaves many people with a sexual ideology of shame and dysfunction.

Therapists carry an internal lens of a "desire for normalcy and for affirmation of their belief that they do not oppress others… preventing many of them from confronting and tolerating these new yet discomforting forms of knowledge. In desiring a sense of normalcy, they [desire] repetition of silence surrounding heterosexism/homophobia" (Kumashiro, 2002, p. 6). Current psychological practices and theories do not hold a space for alternative sexual-relationality. In this respect, therapists treat but they do not heal. Treatment, which works to conform and adjust clients to a norm, stems from a universal model, whereas healing is liberatory, freeing clients from norms and universal modes of living. Healing provides many diverse choices and has no hierarchy of behaviors with which to determine health.

Therapists have become "guardians of normal or socio-politically dominant values" where "the process of locating self relative to social norms quickly [becomes] an automatic and self implemented task for patients" (Hook, 2007, p. 25). Therapists create knowledge and "truth," and as Johnston and Longhurst state, "knowledge is relative to social setting…and the outcome of an active fabrication process rather than the discovery of a reality pre-existent and fully formed" (2009, p. 3). The building of knowledge impacts the loves of clients and our culture. Therapy does not reveal hidden truths, as there is no universal "truth"; rather it constructs and reconstructs the many selves of the client. Psychological models and theories that intersect and critique sex and relationships—such as developmental theories, attachment theory, and evolutionary psychology—ignore the fact that all behavior is embedded within culture, and should therefore be individualized, not built on flawed ideas of an "appropriate" and "expected" trajectory. "Growing sideways versus growing up" (Stockton, 2009, p. 6) brilliantly challenges the idea of mental-social maturation. If you accept that growing sideways is a reasonable mode of growth, it is much easier to see behavior and relationships as a system in constant flux.

Critical therapists point out how therapeutic models and discourses all have an ideological bias and work to sustain certain values, hierarchies, and forms of oppression. Community psychologists report that individual pathology ignores the impacts of community, economics, education, and environment upon an individual's level of functionality. This intersectional approach points out the importance and power of all the many positions and identities individuals occupy. Feminist scholars acknowledge how mental health practices are oppressive to women, as they operate from masculine norms and ignore how much pathology is caused by patriarchy, not individual "female" pathology. They highlight how therapy models posit social pathologies, such as eating disorders and vaginal disorders, as being within the female as opposed to the reality of their being external social creations. Constructivists challenge the idea of science being neutral, calling out the fact that scientists are not independent or uninfluenced by the world around them. And mental health clients challenge the field of psychiatry and the ways diagnoses are punitive and oppressive to diversity, as well as how the field is self-serving, reinforcing all problems as biological and therefore requiring the pharmaceutical cure offered by psychiatry (Parker & Aggleton, 1999, p. 2).

All these theoretical positions and philosophies acknowledge the flaws in the paradigms and grand narratives of current psychology and mental health work. The bottom line is that they all see problems in psychology, for various reasons. All these viewpoints challenge the "therapist as scientist" model that most universities comply with. If psychology as a science were instead seen as theory and not truth or fact, psychology could return to its philosophical roots.

With misinformation, therapists act as dominant cultural figureheads, using their attributed power to force the assimilation of others. The objectivity of science has been proven to be flawed. Science is not immune to racism and sexism (Braidotti, 2013, p. 68). With therapists' current definitions and scales of health, they maintain the culture's desire to fit everyone into a category of "normal." Psychologists and "experts" are given the role of determining the interpretation of arousal responses (e.g., therapists decide whether a man getting an erection during exposure to certain material or experiences is "healthy"). Becker calls this type of person a "moral entrepreneur," someone who creates new or enforces current moral rules (1963, p. 135).

This is how an individual's sexuality is internalized, and that individual gains either sexual confidence or shame about their body, arousal, and eroticism. When a therapist or psychiatrist calls a behavior a "disorder" or "unhealthy," what they are really saying is, "I am anxious or uncomfortable with what you are doing, and so is the rest of society. You must change." This is a passive declaration from the expert that the patient's behavior is incongruent with the expert's own personal model of health—which is both subjective and often arbitrary. I'm not saying there is no relevance to "experts," but good sexual-relational therapy requires a therapist who is free from irrational sex phobias, relates to sex as good, and has an active and abundant sexual life.

Dominici and Lesser frame what one should expect from a metal health expert as such: a respect for diversity, no privilege of one form of sexuality over another, the confrontation of hierarchization, categorization, and use of the concept of "abnormal," exclusion of essentialist views, and seeing identities as cultural productions (1995, p. 5). Our culture as a whole is moving toward a celebration of diversity in certain aspects (race and religious observations, for example), yet within a sexual-relational context, we attempt to snuff out any diversity and call it a cure. Most therapists do not barrage clients who express a desire to marry or be monogamous with a deluge of questions about why and a discussion of the negative consequences, but they definitely do so if you express a preference for non-monogamy or a solo sexual lifestyle. These are all acceptable parts of individuals' sexual arousal constellation and symptoms of healthy sexual diversity and variation—not deviance or disorders to be fixed or cured.

Therapists and therapies act as forms of "micro powers" and are linked to broader forms of power (Hodges, 2008, p. 16). Therapists have the power to shape a client's sense of self and impose limits and boundaries on their autonomy in the world, whereas individuals attend therapy to find freedom and not confinement. Therapy programs and protocols are forms of management and regulation that create a surveillance of behavior. There is a sad bias to treating sexual-relational individuality and rebellion as pathology and disorder.

Within the sexual-therapy world, sex-addiction therapists use anti-sex assessments, assignments, and tools to limit and shame clients, rather than the therapeutic goal of liberation and instilling sexual confidence and health. Therapists help clients create a narrative and a "truth" about their sexual health. But sex-addiction therapists and other sexphobic mental health workers further shame and vandalize already wounded sexual psyches. The tools and assessments of the sex-addiction therapist do *not* find and deal with existing problems but rather invent and create new problems and disorders based on what they perceive to be "wrong" and "unacceptable" sexually. They are not all-knowing sexual messiahs with the keys to sexual health, but are instead uneducated, sexphobic prison guards and appendages of the sex-hating moral code.

The sex-addiction therapy model first creates a vision of sexual health—which happens to be against diversity and alternative sex and relational styles, and obsessively for hetero intercourse and dyadic partner-based sex only—then strives to mold all individuals into this model. The battle cry of "healthy sex can only take place within a relationship" is a lie. There is no universal grand narrative for sexual health that can be applied to all people. Theoretical models are a conventionalizing force of control and mechanism of power. No one holds the truth about sex (the "master reality"), not a sexologist, psychiatrist, or therapist; they all have versions and variations of their own chosen and produced truth. A sexual health–based therapy should help individuals determine their own specific narratives of sexual truth and health. Any method or process that works against sexual freedom is *not* working in service of mental health.

The related sexual twelve-step programs meant to treat sex and love addiction support the internalization of the sex-negative therapeutic mindset. They further reinforce, via the guidance of untrained and non-sexology "sponsors" and "old-timers," a self-policing relationship between self and sexuality. Our culture works hard to distance the self from sexuality and uses programs that further problematize eroticism in all its forms to create sexual anorexia. Sex-negative sex-addiction treatment, coupled with sexual twelve-step programming, aims for the complete annihilation of sexual health, instilling sexual avoidance and fear in its place. These treatments abuse and vandalize creative sexuality and suffocate relational diversity. The sex- and love-addiction concept is a flawed Band-Aid placed over a larger social issue and an attempt at enforcing ideals of sex and relationships. What individuals seek in porn, fantasy, and erotic literature or with extra-relational partners is that which they cannot have in daily life (because sexphobic institutions and policies or our current relational-marital boundaries limit it). This is not an unhealthy seeking, and people should not be shamed for identifying their sexual needs and attempting to secure them.

Many mental health professionals, despite the intention to heal and improve well-being, instead help create and sustain systems of domination and oppression. The therapy acts as an agent for anti-sex morals but poses as science and fact. All therapists must ask about their work: *Does this move people toward shame or toward liberation, freedom, and health? What is the social impact? Increased sexphobia, miseducation, and censorship? Who gets to make the rules? Who is expected to conform? What are the consequences? What values are hidden within? Whose interest does it serve (empower)?* Treatments come from work with dominant groups and promote assimilation into existing problematic structures—structures that created the very problem that now requires resolving.

Therapists act as apparatuses of power, forcing patients to confess their filthy secrets and then disciplining them for doing so. Therapists become a stifling and tyrannical anti-sex superego. Clients come to therapy seeking liberation from social stigma and cultural pressures to conform, but the "expert" winds up restricting the client's freedom through attempts to repress any sexual expression that is different from the norm by framing it as pathological. There are no value-free theories or treatments, and all are situated within power relations. Power and knowledge co-occur with these "experts" who influence norms, knowledge formation, and sexual meanings. Therapeutic work should be liberatory, not further restrictive, as popular culture is already repressive enough. A truly healing and liberation-based therapy must use words like "diverse" and "creative," not "disorder" or "abnormal."

Liberation-centered therapy, which I practice and propose for all therapists, actually does free clients, as opposed to using the sexual body as a vehicle for disciplinary practices. But even though my liberation-centered therapy is actually much healthier for mental development, many individuals fear their own sexual-relational liberation and prefer a prescriptive template to guide them, even if it winds up resulting in a false diagnosis.

Treatment should be both liberating and empowering, and this means pursuing psychotherapy that is about change, both individual and cultural, not about adjustment to how things already are.

Sexual and relational problems are a result of our culture's confining heteronormativity, media influence, sexphobia, gender training, and the Western separate-self model that is anti-relational. My therapy is different because it:

1. Challenges the status quo (normalization is not the goal).
2. Aims to change society by challenging oppression at all levels, contending that mental health is a reflection of one's surroundings. Attention is given to the social conditions from which distress and issues emerge. This means removing, dismantling, and changing what we use to build our psyche. What you read, watch on television, and browse online has an impact on you.
3. Has a relational perspective, which means working on relationships to work on oneself.
4. Acknowledges that all therapy is political, historical, and culturally based. (There are no universal pathologies or identities, as all are culturally and historically bound.)
5. Does not use diagnosis. (Diagnosis sees each individual's behavior as static and consistent. This mistakes situational and contextual behavior as inflexible, ignoring relational and cultural influence and erroneously placing pathology within the individual.)

Liberation-centered therapy allows for the possibility of feeling, thinking, and living authentically.

CHAPTER 5.

THE PRIMACY OF SEXUAL COMPATIBILITY

Sexual compatibility is the most important attribute for relational success, coming before psychological, emotional, and social compatibility. Far too many individuals buy into societal support of love as the only necessary component for relational sustainability, thereby ignoring the best predictor of relational success: sexual desire and congruence. Love is not enough for long-term monogamy or commitment. When love wanes, sexual desire is the required glue that will hold partners together. "Sexual satisfaction is considered to be a barometer for the quality of a relationship" (Sprecher & Cate, 2004, p. 241). As such, waiting to have sex until after marriage or commitment is a template for failure. Sexuality is our most powerful drive and desire, and as such is a crucial tool to use within a relationship. The denial of the power of sex is what drives the couples into my office for sex therapy, as sex issues are implicated in most couples's divorces.

All relationships begin with sexuality. "Problems in romantic relationships have a sexual dimension... Attachment and sex is what coupling is about... Sex is one of the main reasons why we form relationships" (Fonagy, 2009, p. xvii). Sex is the magnet that pulls our gaze toward each other and is what drives individuals to reach out to communicate and connect. Without sex, relationships would never begin. It's sexuality that triggers courtship and holds a couple together through the stages of dating. "The strength and stability of a relationship...depends upon sex... A good sexual relationship creates a unique and powerful form... Sex is the superglue of humanity, meaning that the power of sex in a relationship is its cohesiveness" (Abramson, 2010, p. 35). Without sexuality, life priorities would block any energy put into building a relationship.

THE POWER OF AROUSAL

Romantic and sexual relationships, especially ones containing more than two individuals, are complex and challenging. There are many forces and tensions to pull consorts apart and create a feeling of distance. The availability of sexuality is an antidote to this unwanted space. Nonsexual relational encounters are more likely to "deaden than to renew or reinvigorate the relational field" (Bersani & Phillips, 2008, p. 5).

Sexuality is a bridge to reconnect instantly and can be used in all relationships, after any and all conflicts. The "amazing recuperative powers and life-affirming magic of sexual pleasure" (Tisdale, 1994, p. 16) is necessary for most relationships to be sustainable long term.

When psychological, emotional, or social intimacies have weakened or collapsed, it is sexual attraction and desire that holds healthy couples together. Arousal eclipses minor relational problems and details. Sprecher and Cate cite research reporting that "husbands and wives who say they are sexually satisfied in their marriage are also likely to report high levels of overall satisfaction with their relationship" (2004, p. 241).

Sexual arousal can, thankfully, override psychological issues, because without the healing powers of sex, problems are magnified and feel worse. Far too many couples, while struggling with inter-relational conflicts, do not have sexual intimacy and compatibility to hold them together and are only tethered by the relational title of boyfriend/girlfriend or by a marital contract, and these connectors become oppressive and create resentment. The struggle of why to stay within the troubled relationship begins, and while most can find reasons to stay, that does not build happiness. Healthy people stay in relationships because they are beneficial, pleasurable, and nourishing, not out of obligation, duty, or commitment. Sexual arousal meets these requirements and mitigates the feeling that one might otherwise be held hostage by a commitment.

In research done on long-term happy couples, "sex life is a focus and sexual passion remains central throughout the marriage…although the intensity and frequency of sex may diminish, sex still remains central to their lives" (Wallerstein & Blakeslee, 1995, p. 50). "The best way to ensure a strong emotional and spiritual bond with your spouse is to do the one thing that defines your relationship as different from all others: stay sexually connected" (Weiner Davis, 2003, p. 32). Sexual happiness leads to relational happiness, leading to relational stability, then to relational commitment, then to relational longevity. "When people are asked why they engaged in sexual relationships online, the most common reason given is that they have specific fantasies and desires that are not being fulfilled in their offline relationships" (Ben-Ze'ev, 2004, p. 2).

WAITING FOR SEX

A prevalent cultural myth is that people should wait to have sex, either until they are married or until they are in a committed relationship, and that sex is a vehicle to entice a partner into that commitment. This is backwards logic. Sex should be sought for self-pleasure, not used as a bargaining chip to gain a commitment out of a potential partner. Disappointment occurs when individuals have expectations about what sex will give them. Sex can't be relationally goal-oriented and should not be used as a psychological barter system to garner a spouse, marriage proposal, or long-term commitment. Our culture would like to believe that the final purpose of sex and relationships is lifelong pair bonding and that anything short of this is a failure (Easton & Hardy, 2009, p. 24). But sex can be for the sake of sex. Have sex because you want pleasure! That's its only goal. Stop abusing it with other interests.

Waiting to have sex does *not* make for a healthy relationship and is rarely the right decision. Sex is valid and legitimate, regardless of whether or not it happens within a relationship or a commitment. The best strategy is to have sex based on desire and pleasure. Research shows that "the number one predictor of whether or not a new pairing resulted in a long-term relationship was whether or not both people in the pair were looking for a long-term relationship" (J. Friedman, 2011, p. 145). The evidence of relationships being of poorer quality due to early sexual involvement or starting as a hookup is weak. "Couples who became sexually involved as friends or acquaintances and were open to a serious relationship ended up just as happy as those who dated and waited" ("Study suggests," 2010). The findings show that it's the people themselves and their relational goals, not when sex occurs, that determine relational health and longevity.

Dating is about exploring connection on both sexual and emotional levels. And because a romantic relationship is built and sustained on both physical and psychological levels, long-term sustainable coupling requires the presence of both. "Too often we don't even try at the outset of a relationship to determine whether our partner's sexual style will match our own…we figure love will find a way" (Queen, 2009, p. 27). Committing to a person while only connecting on one level creates flimsy and lopsided relationships that have inherent issues later, such as struggles to maneuver around lack of sexual chemistry. Sex and love are not mutually inclusive, and do not have to ever intersect. Love and lust are different things, and being in love does not guarantee good sex.

Case Study

In my weekly sex therapy group, I meet with people of all genders, sexualities, and relational configurations who are working on their sexual-relational health. The topic of when to be sexual and its impact on a partnership comes up often.

Kevin discussed how he was taught, by his family and the media, that waiting as long as possible to be sexual implied an interest in commitment to a partner and was always best. He said, "If I have sex too soon with the women and men I'm dating, then I'm not taking the time to get to know each of my partners." I explained that learning about another's sexuality is nothing *but* getting to know that person. That waiting actually delays the experience of truly encountering another person at their deepest levels. Sexuality is the best access to another person. And in terms of compatibility and chemistry, it does not just come with other forms of connection, it is its own level of intimacy that needs to be explored prior to commitment. Do not be afraid of sexuality and sexual exploration, as it's through this that many become committed.

Julie reported that her struggle was with her twelve-step sexual-addiction sponsor saying she needed to wait a full year before dating or having sex. I discussed with the group how most people have not received adequate sex education, including a twelve-step sponsor, and as such people tend to perpetuate sexual misinformation. I challenge my sex therapy groups to use their sexuality *as* therapy. Using sex, in all its health and sacredness, to learn about themselves and others is what sex and therapy are for. I taught my group the "Dr. Donaghue 3-Point Rule of Dating Readiness": Date once you have a solid group of friends, you have a career you love, and you are happy. Then you know you are solid enough to date and be dated.

Next in group sex therapy, Ron talked about being extremely attracted to his partner but not having much interest in being sexual with her. I asked him about the type of sex they were having. He replied, "The normal type: penile-vaginal intercourse. But I seem to prefer masturbation and my pornography." We then explored, as a group, the complexity and diversity of arousal constellations, which are all the many parts, themes, situations, and people that arouse us sexually. I reminded the group that there is no "right" form of sex, and that everyone's sexuality is different. Some individuals are more geared toward partnered sex, and others prefer more solo sexuality. Ron's work was going to be to reduce the shame in his sexual preference and orientation toward a more solo sexuality, as well as discussing this with his partner, since she, as his primary sexual partner, was impacted by his sexuality. If they were to stay monogamous, she would have to be given access to sexuality that affirmed her arousal constellation, and as a couple they would have to negotiate how to make everyone's sexuality legitimate and a priority, since neither partner is more important than the other. All sexualities are equally valid.

The group session ended with Christine discussing her discomfort about finding out that her husband uses transsexual pornography as part of his solo sexuality. She asked, "Should I worry that he might be gay? He masturbates to women who have penises. How can I compete with that?" Christine's discomfort and confusion was very intense.

"No, Christine," I told her, "he is not gay, not unless he says so. Your husband, like everyone else, has a diversity to his sexuality. He, and he alone, gets to label and define his sexuality and how he frames his sexual orientation. It's very common for men to enjoy such pornography, even heterosexually identified men." This clarification settled her down. I went on to explain how we are not meant to compete—nor could we—with the vast complexity of another's arousal constellation. That's not what sexual relationships are about.

We ended the group session with the understanding that in a relationship, we cannot police or control a partner's solo sexuality; that is under their control only. They alone get to decide when, how, and to what images they are sexual while alone. We only get to be involved in partnered sex, where we can ask for what arouses us as a couple.

Attachment Theory

Attachment theory has to do with the interpersonal neurobiological connections that occur in romantic partnerships. The affectional-sexual-relational system is a complex web of interactions that determine how safe we feel with our other (in this case, our primary romantic partner) and how we interact with that person. Sexuality is the most important variable within this system. This thread is what weakens or strengthens a couple's sense of safety with togetherness and separateness. Sex gives us the recharge we need to feel safe and close when not with our primary romantic partner, and it also helps us reconnect when they return to us.

Those in the field of psychology are fond of exploring the importance of relational transitions, supporting the use of touch, time together, and eye contact as forms of relational maintenance, but ignoring the healing power of sex as fostering that same kind of connection. The frequent use of eroticism throughout the day is a surefire way to maintain romance and sexuality between partners, and to increase sexual tolerance for those who are avoidant or anxious about sex. To accomplish this, I tell my clients to flirt with each other daily with sexual text messages, picture sharing, sexual touch in passing, or other ways of reminding one another that sex is important and prioritized.

Psychology's sexphobia has left out the acknowledgment that all romantic relationships benefit from continual sexualization.

Applied attachment theory teaches us how sexual behavior harnesses all of our available bonding hormones and neurochemicals and systems in the most intense ways, and allows for the pleasure-connection-intimacy complex to be activated. These chemical reactions are the biological gifts of sex. It's because of this pleasure-bonding cascade system that sex is so important for relational sustainability. Sex provides us with the most competent and successful way to stay connected. Without its bonding capacity, relationships are weakened and struggle for endurance.

The word "sexualization" has been made a pejorative, and is often seen as offensive. But it's really a compliment, as being the object of another's sexuality within the confines of a consensual relationship is both healthy and appropriate. More importantly, it's required for long-term relationships. People should not be shamed for the sharing of their sexual attraction to their partners. The maintenance of sex throughout the day, either by erotic phone calls, sexts, emails, etc., is a needed input for healthy bonding. It's also the best form of foreplay, as it keeps sexuality and arousal always alive and ready to be acted upon.

LOW SEXUAL DESIRE

The issue of low sexual desire is the most common relational problem. One of the solutions is sexual compatibility. Individuals have differing levels of sex drive, and finding a partner with congruence and tolerance of yours will help you avoid some future problems. If more couples paid attention to sexual desire congruence and maintained sexuality continually, sexual disconnection and diminishment would not occur. A maxim of sexology is: "The more you have sex, the more you have sex." Sex is an active system that increases with activity. If individuals put as much time and effort into satisfying their sexual needs as they do their social and emotional ones, sex would never drop off the radar. Imagine a couple saying that now that they are married or have a child, they've decided that a verbal connection is no longer important so they have stopped having conversations. The removal and avoidance of sex from a relationship is just as ridiculous, yet it's very commonplace. For many, marriage and long-term relationships mean "unlimited, enthusiastic sex with someone they fancy. The absence of sex is felt keenly as a breach of promise, and a personal rejection" (Hakim, 2012, p. 44).

A common misunderstanding occurs with the concepts of sexual attraction versus romantic attraction. These two experiences do not always coincide, and with the absence of one, a relationship can feel depriving or unsatisfying. Many individuals feel romantically drawn toward a partner, enjoy spending time with him or her, are open to affection, yet have no desire for eroticism or sex. This can be confusing, as the strong romantic interest creates a drive toward partnering or marriage, yet lack of sexual attraction or chemistry leaves a void in the couples' intimacy and connection. Choosing monogamy without sexual attraction is the cause of many marital-relational issues.

EROTIC RISK

Sex is the best vehicle for self-exploration and to work on oneself (in addressing self-esteem, communication, boundaries, intimacy, body esteem, relational traumas, and more). Sex is a learned capacity, and sexual partners can help challenge and push us in that development.

Healthy relationships allow for the examination of one's eroticism, and especially one's preferred level of erotic risk. This is where one allows sexual boundaries to be expanded and challenged in the service of pleasure and sexual growth. It involves a willingness to have one's psyche disturbed and opened to ideas, images, and behaviors that enlarge one's psychic capacity.

Relationships require going into the dark depths of why we choose what we choose sexually and relationally, and through this, we risk having to grow. All sexual-relational configuration choices have costs and benefits.

"People have sex to the limits of their development" (Schnarch, 2009, p. 164). If a form of sexuality makes someone feel anxious, then he will avoid it, which limits the sexuality of his partner, stunts his own growth, and leads to boredom. Good, healthy sex *should* make you anxious. I challenge my clients to use sex as a way to gain more closeness and intimacy, by pushing into areas that communicate to their partners that they value them, their relationship, and their sexual pleasure. How we have sex and the kind of sex we have shows our partners who we are.

SEXUAL SCRIPT INCONGRUENCE

One of the most disruptive dynamics within relationships and marriage is incongruent sexual styles and interests. Many people erroneously prioritize psychological connection, as though sexual connection is irrelevant. The importance of dating is the exploration and enjoyment of partners emotionally and socially, but most importantly sexually, because "sexuality requires chemistry" (Mitchell, 2002, p. 61)—not love, not friendship, not security, but chemistry.

It takes sexual experience to explore the presence or nonexistence of passion. As a sex therapist, I am able to aid partners in points of erotic intersection, where commonalities exist, but I cannot help create chemistry and passion where they do not exist. I can help clients reconnect sexually, but I cannot help build something that never existed. In these cases, the therapy is about either creating new outlets for each partner to have access to the sex they desire and challenging each other to expand the tolerance of their arousal boundaries to incorporate new behaviors, or mourning the loss of highly arousing sex within their current relationship.

SEXUAL COMPATIBILITY

Sexual compatibility is about interest in and tolerance for what arouses each partner. It's built from the interactions of sexual attitudes, sexual desires, and sexual frequency. These are not exclusive categories, but they frequently intermingle and intersect. Together they form the basis of a couple's expected daily interactions with sexuality. Our arousal constellations are built from internal unconscious processes that are out of our control as well as external sexual-social fields that are the internalization and imitation of the collective sexual life we embed ourselves in socially (A. Green, 2014, p. 5). Our sexualities are fluid and have the ability to expand and encompass new things that we previously found non-erotic.

Sexual compatibility encompasses the following:

1. Sexual Attitudes

The sexual health levels of each partner, as demonstrated by sexual confidence or sexphobia, will begin to map out sexual compatibility. How individuals speak about sex, the words used and their comfort with them, begins to provide clarification of what to expect sexually. How people talk about sex speaks to how they feel about it, in terms of its importance and to what degree they see sex as healthy and positive. In addition, sexual attitudes lead to the sexual boundaries set by each partner, as well as how the crossing of those boundaries is dealt with. My advice is to always go into relationships and sexual encounters with full-on sexual confidence about your desires. Never allow another's sexual anxieties to diminish or shame your interests. As discussed earlier, sex is the best container within which to grow and work on yourself. Do not take responsibility for managing a partner's anxiety around your sexuality.

2. Sexual Desires

The next level of compatibility is based upon similarity and tolerance for what each partner is aroused by. There are no right or wrong arousals, just ones that are congruent or incongruent with a given potential partner. Because of the vast complexity of arousal constellations, there will hopefully be many points of intersection between any two people. It is possible for partners and couples who are deeply in love to match on only a few minor levels. These couples will struggle to find long-term relational happiness and sexual pleasure if they maintain their sexuality within such a limited system. If sex is to be prioritized and valued, an interest in or openness to one another's sexual scripts is necessary. Neither party's sexual constellation should be prioritized or legitimized over the other, as sexual appropriateness and acceptability cannot be ranked; all sexualities are valid in sexually healthy and mature couples.

3. Sexual Frequency

The final point, and the most highly charged, is the frequency at which individuals desire to be sexual. The management of this is another window into a couple's health. Healthy sexual partners do not manage one another's disparate sexual desires with shame or contempt. Being the object of someone else's sexual desire is the goal of romantic-sexual coupling. It's what pushes individuals beyond friendship and platonic boundaries. Being approached by a partner for sex is a compliment and sign of being eroticized by them. This is a requirement for long-term coupling.

There is no correct level of sexual desire, and as such it is no more appropriate to adjust to the lower-desiring partner's sexual interest than to the higher-desiring partner. However, for those choosing the option of sexual monogamy, it is sexually abusive and aggressive to want to own your partner's sexuality and to be their only source for partnered sex, but then refuse to have sex with them. Everyone has a right to long-term sexuality. Monogamy is not a healthy configuration for couples who have disparate sexual interests and desires.

CHAPTER 6.

THE FANTASY OF MARRIAGE

Marriage isn't in crisis; marriage *is* the crisis. Tradition-ally, marriage has been assumed to be the choice for people in love who are truly committed and want intimacy with nobody else. Yet not all relationships can be or are meant to be long term. The problem is that as a society, we are culturally afraid to explore the costs of clinging to a single relationship model that all of us are supposed to be working toward. We need to examine the ways we practice marriage. We must begin to critique marriage so we can understand the ways it is powerfully different from love, commitment, and intimacy.

Marriage creates a biological and social double bind. There's the tension of wanting to bond with someone else as a pair while also wanting autonomy. There's also a desire for both psychological commitment and somatic freedom. Statistics show that we are not built to navigate this tension successfully. Rates of adultery, divorce, and opting to stay single are at historic highs. But the problem isn't with the people who are getting married. The problem is with the institution itself.

> [Marriage] is a function of our social rather than our personal consciousness; it compels married people to abide by external values, to participate in a generic rather than individual or visionary consciousness... We become like sheep... The truth is marriage—as a relationship—has been appropriated by society, and as it serves society, it

> often suffocates the individual… We let our marriages become watered-down versions of values of society. (Kingma, 1998, p. 31)

As it currently exists, marriage is the worst decision someone can make for relationship success. This is why half of all marriages end in divorce and a high percentage of those that do last aren't fulfilling. Relationships require love, commitment, and intimacy to survive. The marital contract creates none of this, instead allowing partners to stop doing the necessary work to be better versions of themselves and to merely let the laziness of the contract to hold them together. The arduousness of the divorce process keeps many trapped in toxic marriages. Couples need both the freedom to leave when they want to and the tension of this freedom to keep them bringing their best to a relationship.

THE MYTH OF MARRIAGE

In both my clinical practice and my social life, I watch most couples struggle within the confines of their marital vows. I believe strongly in the concept of boundaries, as they help us build trust, manage partner expectations, and construct relational identities. Where so many couples get into trouble with marriage is the unconscious collusion with externally assumed and internalized rules. They fall victim to an assumed structure of what is "healthy" and "right." Few recognize the parts of marriage where we can exercise our own choices.

While often seen or defined as "natural," marriage is just a social creation originally established to secure ownership of women and children and thereby guarantee the inheritance of property. Its early history is linked to state control over private property (Ingraham, 2005, p. 7). "Marriages sought to merge the property and good name of families to ensure economic well-being and the perpetuation of family status and prestige" (Rice, 1996, p. 96). The needs a marriage contract met at the time of its conception are no longer powerful variables ruling our lives. We are all far more individualistic, empowered, and economically stable. The rigid expectations of lifetime commitment, dyadic monogamous sexual style, and gender role maintenance have eroded to allow a more individualistic and flexible sexual-relational option set.

Marriage carries with it many myths about what is functional and sustainable. In the decade of my marital-sexual-relational clinical work, I have seen many individuals and couples buckling under the weight of misconceptions about what is "healthy," and what their vision should be for their relationship. For relationships to survive and flourish, individuals need to recognize the multitude of options available to them and be supported in their exploration and choices of what is appropriate for them. Our history of two relational options—single or committed (monogamous)—is archaic. Institutions are meant to serve us, not the other way around.

Marriage has always been about economic privilege. It's just the definitions of what those privileges are that have changed. In addition to human-rights-based equality, other sexual identities want access to marriage for specific benefits. In order to acquire these privileges, couples must give up their autonomy and self-agency, ignore whatever diversity might be occurring between them, and be forced into an outmoded configuration meant to last the rest of their lives. If one is not interested in this single relational option, or in registering their relationship with the state for legitimacy, then their relationship is deemed illegitimate. What defines a couple should not be regulated and decided by the government, but by the individuals themselves. Either the designation of "marriage" should be applied to any relationship as the individuals choose it, or the specific benefits of marriage (such as health care) should be available to everyone. We don't need to be more liberal about marriage and relationships—we need to be radical!

The relationships we engage in make up both our intrapersonal and interpersonal worlds. We are all many selves, and all these aspects of who we are require a multitude of relationships and others to validate, confirm, and nourish them. Socialization is repeatedly documented to be a mood-enhancing, life-affirming, and psychologically necessary experience. When we allow marriage to remove or limit our access to connections with others, we deny our many different identities. Many people allow marriage to bring about the loss of their other selves and relationships, collapsing all their various identities into one relational identity labeled "husband" or "wife." This is a suppression of the many selves we can play—family member, brother, sister, best friend, coworker, artist, etc.—and often leads to a depressive loneliness and sense of loss. Each of our many identities are important and deserve recognition and actualization.

A marriage should not obliterate one's prior self. I urge my clients to say, "Honey, I love you, but I need to do things that define who I am outside of this partnership." I suggest using different nights of the week to nurture different identities, i.e., Wednesdays can be girls' night out, Thursdays can be for art classes, Sundays for spending time alone, and Mondays and Saturdays can be reserved for couple time. Marriage should have the capacity to expand and fit more people and activities inside it, enlarging one's life instead of shrinking it.

Another part of our life that can be damaged by marriage is sexuality. Sex is the most important part of long-term sustainable relationships for those who choose monogamy. Sexual arousal requires another person to be attracted to. The initial relational drive is to treat your partner like a drug. Once intimacy is established, a loss of sexual interest is inevitable. Many see marriage, the ultimate expression of one's intimacy with another, as a loss of personal boundaries, a merging of two into one. Without another person in your relationship, your highly arousing sexual life disappears.

Do not underestimate the importance of building and maintaining a sex life in a successful marriage. Sadly, sex is often undervalued compared with other forms of intimacy, even though so many of the ways people connect with one another—intimacy tolerance, partner interest, compatibility, and level of commitment—are driven by our sexuality.

Traditional marriage can block our abilities to express healthy levels of sexual arousal due to the misunderstanding that "healthy" or "good" relationships should be parasitic. The way marriage is commonly understood in our society, a "healthy" couple is always tethered to each other, never separated for too long, and closed to outside relationships of any kind. But in reality, separation and distance allow for optimal relational functioning and encourage sustainable sexuality. Sexual desires and drives are part of human functioning, and they need to be given appropriate space for expression and engagement.

Emotional health is the final part of the trifecta impacted by marriage. Many feel that marital commitment is the only and truest form of expressing love, yet marriage implies nothing about one's level of romantic interest. Many unmarried couples have far more love and commitment than married ones, while many married couples have far less interest and love. As a result, I refer to any connection with another person—whether you're married, dating, monogamous, or with various levels of commitment—as a relationship, in order to honor every couple's preferences and to show that any kind of connection with another human being requires work.

The cultural and social brainwashing that leads people to think marriage is the goal of any connection between two people can seriously impact your emotional health. Dating can lead to finding a marital or long-term partner, but it can also be about socialization, meeting new people, having consistent sexual partners, or strictly for recreation. When you accept society's rules about what dating and marriage should mean, you rob yourself of autonomy and self-agency.

Healthy adults do not partake in limiting and self-deprecating inherited belief systems. They critically analyze beliefs and institutions they engage in and create boundaries that meet their own chosen goals. This is the powerful moment when you literally throw away the rulebooks. Get rid of any guide or program for how to date. Your emotional health requires you to learn to make decisions based on who you are at each moment in time, with each new person, and within each new relationship. Remember, we are many selves that are always changing, and we are different within each different relationship. The self that worked with one person won't necessarily work with someone new.

The institution of marriage is in need of a great deal of updating and reconfiguring. There are no relational facts about what marriage is, just versions of the institution that we have made habits of and which therefore feel like truths. Marriage is a man-made institution, and like all human theories, it's up to you to decide as an individual what form it should take for you and your partner. Treat marriage as malleable, and allow your individual relationship choices to give it its shape.

The current marriage model erroneously demands that your relationship be: "daily (seven days a week), domestic (lived under a shared roof), exclusive (the person we love will be our one and only), and forever (last until the end of time)" (Kingma, 1998, p. 33). These myths, based on antiquated and damaging gender expectations, should be disregarded. Gender in particular is a topic that often creates conflict. Many friends or therapists erroneously collude with traditional gender roles by helping the couple adjust to the assumed normal gender roles, such as the man working while the woman focuses on child-rearing.

We need to help balance and renegotiate these rules, because none of them are necessary, required, or inherently healthy or functional. Many unconscious unexamined contracts are made about the roles each partner will assume. The concepts of "lifetime commitments," "role fulfillment," and "soul mates" can guilt us into forgetting that marriage is a contract and, like all contracts, negotiable.

THE FLAWED CONCEPT OF SOUL MATES

One of the more damaging concepts I hear about in my practice and within our culture is the soul mate. Although most of us know how flawed it is to look for or believe in this supernatural nonexistent being, the magical thinking of manifesting an omnipotent creation that can solve all our dissatisfactions still lingers. In our search for the soul mate we make lists of required qualities, envision ideal partners, and create vision boards, all of which reek of inflexibility and fantasy-based notions of the other. Instead of trying to fulfill your needs, the search for a soul mate allows you to focus solely on your wants. This can be the enemy of having a successful relationship.

Relational work is about being open and confident with ambiguity. Start now by allowing your partner the space to be who they are, not the idealized version of who you want them to be. The work is not about your partner becoming someone else but about who *you* want to be within each relationship. When relationships fail, it's often due to one partner's inability to tolerate who the other person is and what it means to be in a relationship with him or her. With a high enough tolerance, almost every relationship that's not emotionally or physically abusive can work out. Use your current relationship to grow and increase your tolerance. All relationships suffer impacts from prior relationships. This is why it's important to always work through issues instead of searching for a magical soul mate to solve all your problems.

Every relationship is an active system, meaning it is constantly responding to the participants in it and the society around it. Humans are highly flexible and sensitive to who they relate to. By raising the bar for how you are acting in a relationship, you can influence how your partner or partners act. My relational mantra is: *Keep the bar high for yourself*. In doing so, you'll also be raising it for those around you.

When I am working with a couple, I use a video monitoring setup to demonstrate my theory. After the session, I edit out one member of the couple to emphasize that while we are all impacted by those we're in relationships with, we can only accept responsibility for our own contributions and choices. I hold my clients accountable for all the choices they make, regardless of what their partner did before or after. This is why soul mates, even if they existed, aren't necessary if you're living your life the way you should. The implication behind "the one" is that they wouldn't require us to monitor our own behavior. The fantasy is that a soul mate would never frustrate us, make us have to regulate ourselves, or create conflict. But the very nature of being in a relationship means having to deal and cope with another person. Individuals are expected to grow in disparate directions. That's a basic part of psychological and sociological development.

Partner choice can be confusing due to society's need to define emotional connection as the primary component in a marriage. We're told, "Don't be superficial and judge someone's looks." I say the opposite. Physical attraction and sexual compatibility are healthy and viable decision-making tools. Sexual arousal is a great guide to starting a relationship. Choosing a partner based on sexual compatibility is as important if not more so than choosing one based on emotional connection. There are times in all relationships when we feel emotionally disconnected or neglected and the power of sexual attraction is needed to keep us close and committed. Likewise, during periods of less sex or sexual struggles, we need emotional compatibility to be the glue in our relationship.

"The one" and "soul mate" concepts infantilize the adult process of growing and learning in relationships with others. Understanding the necessary flexibility of relationship boundaries as well as the impracticality of expecting a relationship to last forever leaves one needing to focus on attraction, then on courting and learning, followed by moving into stages of commitment if interested. Dating is not a commitment or a promise. It's an investigation into the compatibility levels of another person via entertainment, sexuality, and companionship.

ALL CONTRACTS CAN BE RENEGOTIATED

The biggest lie of all is this: *I promise to love you and be with you forever.*

Future-oriented thinking and commitments are all based in fantasy. We never know where—or, more importantly, *who*—we'll be in the future. We only know how we feel right now. Thus, we can only commit to being the person we are right now. Committing to the concept of "forever" means agreeing that you're always going to be the same person. That isn't possible.

Taking this a step further, an honest expression of the marriage contract would be: *I love and commit to you now, but if or when that changes, I commit to letting you know so we can renegotiate this arrangement.* Not doing this creates a relational hostage situation. The goal of relationships is not bondage or slavery (unless that's erotic to you and your partner), but an addition to and expansion of oneself and one's life. There is no valor in maintaining connections that are draining or negatively impacting you. Marriage can often be too much of a commitment, so much so that individuals often stay even when a partner refuses to evolve and grow. The myth of "forever" is not congruent with reality. "It most likely will take more than one relationship and perhaps even several marriages (particularly as we live longer and longer) to get you to the one person who will be there on the scene when you breathe your last breath" (Kingma, 1998, p. 40).

Psychologically healthy people evolve and have ever-changing wants and desires. The relationships that serve us now may not in the future. The most loving act you can commit in a relationship is to let the other person know immediately when your wants and desires change. Otherwise you are holding on to unnecessary secrets or creating useless boundaries. This leads to resentment and, more importantly, becomes a serious blockade to further relational intimacy. Low sexual desire, dissipated relational passion, and the general malaise of a long-term commitment are built upon the shoulders of not continually deepening levels of one's relational intimacy. The comfort a static couple's status quo provides, along with a desire for long-term stability, is so strong that many will not risk the needed shot of reality and conflict to work toward a better relationship. Redefining relational boundaries, challenging partners to engage in a diversified sexuality, and revealing one's struggle with an expired marriage contract are all cultural acts of courage within our codependent culture, as well as being necessary behaviors for personal evolution. This kind of work leads to better functioning of both familial and social relationships.

Culturally we have forgotten the difference between a commitment and martyrdom. Commitment means staying in a relationship when both partners are doing their work. Martyrdom is keeping yourself in a relationship even when it has been shown to be unhealthy, hostile, or oppressive. Cases of abuse and mental trauma are immediate situations where a relationship or a marriage should be renegotiated.

When marriage is renegotiated in an abusive relationship—ideally by voiding the contract altogether—partners have to improve their behavior for their own sake and not because a contract says they should. If a partner can leave a marriage at any time, then each partner has to behave in a way that prevents complacency from dissolving commitment and love. Do you want your relationship and commitment to be based on love or obedience?

Kate: A Case Study

Kate had been in a committed monogamous relationship for many years. She was unhappy with her sex life because she had allowed her partner's sexuality to determine how they would be sexual as a couple, including what behaviors were allowed and where/when they had sex.

"I feel as though I have abandoned a huge part of myself," she said. "Not being able to have the type of sex that arouses me makes me feel resentful and empty."

I explained to Kate that she *should* feel this way. Abandoning her full sexuality is both an act of low self-esteem and a loss of integrity. We discussed how entering into a monogamous relationship ideally means using sex as a way to grow and deepen your relationship with your partner. Kate wasn't having that kind of experience.

"My partner is unwilling to try new sexual things and I cannot imagine this being the way I have sex for the rest of my life," she said.

Kate had allowed her anxiety about asking for the type of sex she wanted to run her relationship. Anything that makes her anxious is exactly where her psychological and relational work lies. Kate explored what scared her about asserting her sexual desires and making them as legitimate as her partner's. She decided that she needed to discuss this struggle with her partner because she could not be in a relationship that didn't prioritize her sexuality.

Sex is the perfect place for individuals to "grow up." Abandoning sex or sexual variety to avoid situations that create anxiety is oppressive; this is what leaves a partner searching for other outlets for pleasure. Monogamy and other chosen sexual boundaries and agreements are a commitment to work with who your partner is sexually. It's not about limitations. If a couple is unwilling to grow sexually and honor both partners' sexuality, then monogamy is not right for them and will lead to frustration and disappointment. The goal of commitment agreements, such as monogamy and marriage, is not to create a sexual hostage situation but to serve as a promise of intimacy and care, neither of which existed for Kate.

HONESTY IS NOT THE BEST POLICY

We live in a sexually anxious culture that comfortably stigmatizes past or current sexual behavior. As such all relationships, including marriage, need to allow for boundary-setting around what is shared and communicated. The fluctuation between privacy and transparency is a learning process. Being healthy means you don't need to share all of your sexual history with others. One mantra I pass along to my clients is: *Never share how many sexual partners you've had*. Many new partners ask this question as an attempt to determine one's dateability. Being a sex-positive and sexually confident person means never apologizing for your sexual history. New partners get access to that part of your life only if you feel it's safe and constructive to share and that it won't be used against you. Your partner doesn't have ownership over all your thoughts and feelings, and people who respect themselves don't give that ownership away. No one has a right to know everything about you, your history, or all your sexual behaviors.

When considering privacy within relationships, one needs to determine what kind of impact various disclosures will have. Suggesting that "honesty is the best policy" is not a psychologically sound philosophy. This is because many relationships are structured in a way that prioritizes avoiding any anxiety or conflict. If true intimacy is prioritized, then ideas and desires are shared that make you and your partner anxious in service of growth and truly being known.

The impact on the self and the other is always the top consideration when making disclosures. The point isn't to relieve guilt, but to foster a situation that allows the couple to get closer, bond more strongly, and learn to have mature conversations. This is both intrapersonal and interpersonal work. If sharing or making a disclosure will enhance a relationship, allow one to be better understood or known, or give a partner the data they need to have the freedom to make a choice, only then is it the right thing to do.

One of the more common questions about honesty in a relationship involves sexual interactions with new people—i.e., cheating. Traditionally, one is expected to always come clean and be honest about this behavior. But depending on the relationship's current state or the functioning level of the partner, this can be a painful or traumatizing experience.

If the relationship is already being renegotiated, or if the partner is not in a grounded/healthy state to be able to tolerate hearing an intimate disclosure, then an external sexual relationship shouldn't be shared because it will most likely cause pain without offering any insight or enlightenment. The partner who cheated, however, does have a responsibility to use this opportunity to learn about themselves.

How do you determine whether to reveal an infidelity to your partner? In general, if the cheating was a one-time issue, won't bleed into the relationship in other ways, and can be used as an opportunity to work therapeutically on renegotiating boundaries or improving partner intimacy, the information should be kept private. However, if the relationship evolves to a place where the partner who has been cheated on can likewise learn from the experience, then the infidelity could be shared in a constructive way. Disclosing having cheated can enhance the primary relationship if both partners are emotionally healthy enough to discuss it, as it can highlight unmet needs. Relationships with too much distance may need more closeness, or relationships with low-level sex may need increased sexuality.

Today's relationship climate is full of long-term monogamy-based commitments. We often don't realize how brave and powerful a decision monogamy is to make. Just like any other relationship style (open, polyamorous, etc.), monogamy requires a lot of communication and mature conversations, those hard-to-have yet crucial discussions that build intimacy. A good way to start conversations like this would be, "This is hard for me to say, and I know it will be hard for you to hear, but I need to share with you."

These conversations are built from a place of anxiety. This is a good thing. Anxiety is a cornerstone in building intimacy. If what you are sharing and discussing with your partners does not make you anxious, then you are not building intimacy, but instead choosing to remain unknown and superficial.

Case Study: Conner

Conner was a broken man, overwhelmed with shame because he constantly had sex outside of the monogamous boundaries that he and his wife had chosen for themselves. Conner broke into tears as he explained how much he loved his wife, yet he was frequently having sex with other women while traveling for work. His wife, who didn't know about his multiple sex partners, wanted to know why he was entering therapy.

"We tell each other everything," he told me. "But I'm not sure how to tell her about this. I don't want to lie to her. What should I say?"

Conner elaborated that his marriage was doing poorly and his wife was depressed. I asked him how he thought sharing his cheating would impact himself, his wife, and their relationship. He explained that no part of his life was currently healthy or strong enough to tolerate such a disclosure at the moment.

I explained to Conner the concept "intimacy bombs." The purpose of sharing information is to connect with our partner and deepen our relationship. We do not just share information impulsively without considering how it will impact us and those around us. If discussing sex you're having outside your primary relationship won't be constructive or helpful in that moment, then it's a "bomb." You should not drop intimacy bombs.

My advice was: "You have to enact privacy in a loving and supportive way. Explain to your wife that you are currently in therapy to work on parts of yourself that you're not okay with and are not helping you have the relationship you want with her. Let her know that after you do some work you'll tell her what you were working on, so that she and the relationship can benefit."

HEALTHY MARRIAGE

A healthy marriage is one filled with freedom and love. It's not a toxic hostage situation, nor is it a "one option only" ritual or commitment. A healthy marriage is one in which partners have honestly individualized and tailored their boundaries to best fit each other. Commitments are active processes that never reach a finalized state. Relationships are highly active systems, and as such they will have constantly changing requirements.

Healthy relationships are built from personal boundaries instead of externally enforced margins. Boundaries are contextual, fluid, and relative to a specific couple at a specific moment. Those boundaries are negotiated solely by the couple, not inherited from society or the state. There is more safety, pleasure, and freedom in an arrangement in which both parties know they have self-chosen their own boundaries and as such can maintain autonomy and control over their future together. Pre-fabricated "one size fits all" contracts should create a fear of commitment, as they are an attempt to ignore the situational and evolving desires of an individual and a couple based on their relationship trajectory. Fixed and rigid margins, in the end, only promote relationship instability.

Without the possibility of change and renegotiation, marriages become psychologically and sexually abusive. Couples need to create their own rules, norms, and boundaries. Stringent divorce laws need to be abolished.

CODEPENDENCE IS HEALTHY

Our culture has an intimacy disorder. We shame and pathologize closeness, dependency, and connection. Our most important developmental goal should be the ability to build and maintain intimate relationships. Psychological health is determined by relationships and human connections. This relational ability, dependence, is far more important and needed than independence. Yet, particularly in the United States, our cultural ideals support individualism, competition, and independence.

My clinical work with couples is about helping them find the "*us*" in their relationships. This is a relational practice that moves them away from a self-centered mode of thinking. Finding the *us* is when both partners connect and grow as individuals while also focusing on the development of one another and the partnership.

Marriages fail due to the prioritization of individuality and separate self ideals, gender roles, and heteronormative models of functioning. All human development takes place *within* relationships, not with just the self.

Making and maintaining relationships is the primary task of infancy, adolescence, and adulthood—all of life. Yet sadly, children are torn away from primary caregivers with the destructive myth that growth and maturity only occurs in disconnection. This model of devaluing relationship sets up adults to not value relationship and deep intimacy later in life, and to avoid or have anxiety about intimacy and dependence. Being trained to be an agent of disconnection serves no one. Healthy, sustainable relationships are not born from inwardly focused, independent people. Such traits breed disconnection, distance, and isolation. They are the traits that drive couples into my clinical practice because of the resultant depression, loneliness, lack of sex, and narcissism. Such separate-self-focused traits perpetuate dominance and competitiveness, not the required mutuality and collaboration all marriages and relational commitments need.

Our mainstream model is one of movement from dependence to independence, and this separate self is promoted culturally as the goal of mature adult development. But the final goal of development is into interpersonal relationships, not away from them. Western culture is far too comfortable honoring relational detachment as the mark of maturity and adulthood. In fact the opposite is true, and this magical, socially constructed self exists only while connecting with and relating to others. As relationships grow and expand, so do the individuals within them. Human growth occurs when people challenge themselves and expand to empathize and understand others' experiences. This leads to the understanding of marriage and relationships as based in mutuality, not fairness. Relationships cannot be equal or fair, but mutuality implies respect for all partners. This means sharing resources and power and valuing differences.

Gender training and socialization often set up men to struggle the most. Typically men are not taught to find self-worth in creating and maintaining relationships, but instead are trained to seek value primarily in productivity, achievement, and financial success, all of which are isolated, solo pursuits. The mental and relational health of individuals is severely vandalized by traditional gender-role socialization. The convention of males trained to value independence and achievement at the expense of relationships and intimacy building kills marriages, as does the perpetuation and support of this sexism by women.

Basic interpersonal neurobiology explains how "there are no single brains." All brains require relationships to both form and continue to function. Each brain is dependent on loved ones for its survival, growth, and well-being. The brain is an organ of adaption that builds its structures through interactions with others. A single human brain does not exist. Without mutually stimulating interactions, people and neurons wither and die. The brain requires a community of other brains: relationships are our natural habitat (Cozolino, 2006, pp. xvi; 4).

This is misunderstood when we pathologize those who appear to overemphasize relationships. Freud, Jung, Erickson, Piaget, and all the forefathers of autonomy and individual "selves" had it wrong! Codependence is a functional drive from humans; autonomy is not. In fact, the most damaging psychological state is isolation. The ways we strive to avoid being relational are where our relational and psychological work lies. These strategies *are* our relational-marital issues. We live in a culture that is happy to promote individualism; your work lies in countering this. "We now can add a corollary to Darwin's survival of the fittest: Those who are nurtured best survive best" (Cozolino, 2006, p. 7).

The sign of psychological health is not a separate self, individuation, or autonomy, but relational engagement that is sustained and mutuality enhancing. I provide my clients and friends with this shorthand psychological test to use for partner assessment when asked out on a date: Ask a potential suitor if he is still friends with his exes, and how his last relationships ended. The way he describes his ex, the way things were left, and how he relates to that person now will all help describe his psychological and relational health.

RELATIONAL ESTEEM

What is needed in relationships is not more differentiation, not more self-sufficiency and self-reliance, but relational sufficiency and reliance. We must move from separate self-esteem to relational esteem. Self-esteem is built in relationship to others. Most differentiation- and separation-based relational myths, psychological models, and social advice teach that we are healthier and stronger if we can exist without connection to another person. "Psychology itself, with its reigning separate-self paradigm, its overemphasis on individualism, and its emphasis on independent 'doers' reinforces this sense of separateness" (Jordan, 2004a, p. 49). In my therapy groups I remind clients that we are all always in relationships. It is nearly impossible to exist outside of them, as even when we are alone we are still symbolically, and with memory and thought, driven and influenced by our relationships.

With our ever-present drive to relate, the denial of this in service of being healthy and single is a myth. I promote the idea that our psychological work only takes place when we are in relationships. We grow in and toward relationships, not away from them. When clients say "I'm taking time to work on myself," I explain that working on oneself only happens with relational work, as we are relational beings. Working on oneself while solo is easy and lazy, and is an actual avoidance of doing the real work. It is others that challenge us to be better and to see ourselves more clearly; when we're solo, there is no work to be done, as we are at our safest. When you are "getting in touch with yourself" and focused only on your own development, others in your life take second and third place.

The psyche and the individual do *not* exist apart from social relationships. Individualism and autonomy are forms of hiding out. Development occurs in relationship and not through separation from others. Relational esteem is about discovering one's worth through being part of meaningful relationships that have mutuality, where both individuals' lives are enhanced. Japanese Amae psychology, transcultural psychology, feminist-based theory, and multitudes of other philosophies and praxis support the idea that a Western, white, male model of "separation," where autonomy is prioritized, is actually racist, sexist, and damaging. Other cross-cultural psychologies value a more relational perspective. They promote ideals of "no self" and pathology as isolation and separation from relationships, valuing what Western psychology would call "codependence." It is arrogant, abusive, and naïve to treat those with a greater ability for or interest in closeness or attachment as fused, codependent, or poorly boundaried. Self-actualization requires relational actualization, not self-reliance. Self-worth and self-esteem can be created within relationships. Both sexual and relational health lie in relational quality and functioning—its process, not its structure and form.

Another therapist once described to me a session where she shamed a family for supporting their child in sleeping in bed with them, because she said the child would not learn to self-soothe and build autonomy. Hers is a common view, as "traditional theories are of 'self-out-of-relationship' or 'self-partly-in-relationship'" (Bergman, 1991, p. 3). This is racist and ethnocentric thinking. Anthropologists and transcultural psychologists report that in many other cultures, especially in India, it's the norm for parents to allow children to sleep in bed with them. So why, when faced with this idea, do we not value alternatives but instead presume pathology?

> The psychological description of the world has been written predominantly by white, middle-class men from Western cultures… Their experiences are reflected in society's theories of individual development… They maintain that any way of relating to the world other than that of

> male, singularly defined accomplishment of separation and individuation is unhealthy. In contrast, people in all of the undervalued groups (women, people with disabilities, people of color, gays and lesbians, working class, etc.) have developed interdependence as a way of life... Those who see "independence" as the only healthy option may not be taking into account the practices and values of the majority of the world. (D. Green, 1990, pp. 91, 92)

"It is not only culturally insensitive but also unethical to impose one group's standards of what constitutes emotional health and well-being onto another group" (Contratto, 2002, p. 33). The qualities that the U.S. mental health system define as "healthy" are those associated with traditional male socialization.

The developmental model practiced and taught in all American universities and by a majority of psychologists theorizes that "human development proceeds by separation from the primary caregiver (mother) toward an ideal stage of 'autonomy' characterized by a rigidly separate, self-sufficient self" (Greenspan, 1993, p. xxiii). But this is far from a universal model for development and health. It again leaves out the theories and behaviors of other cultures and periods of history. This developmental model universalizes that which cannot be universalized; ignores cultural, historical, and political differences; and assumes that all sexualities, races, genders, classes, and groups have the same path. It creates a "norm" that makes anything creative or diverse a deviation and disorder. It is this very idea that creates the need for most couples therapy.

If individuals, especially males in our culture, were raised with a relational model that values the other and sees self-esteem and health in the quality of relationships one builds and how one operates within them, then intimacy issues, emotional avoidance, violence, and most conflict would cease to exist. Healthy development is not about separation (child from parent, self from other) but about transforming the relationship and the way two people relate. In fact, much trauma occurs when parents erroneously follow the dictate that boys must separate emotionally from their mothers in order to mature.

> Mothers are encouraged to separate from their sons, and the act of forced separation is so common that it is generally considered to be "normal." But I have come to understand this forcing of early separation is so acutely hurtful to boys that it can only be called a trauma—an emotional blow of damaging proportions… All kids separate at their own rates and…boys need not be pushed to separate more quickly than girls. (Pollack, 1998, pp. 12; 23)

Relational maintenance serves young girls *and* boys, as it teaches the needed tools for later adult relationships. Relationships are to be maintained but reprioritized with new forms. Leaving a current relationship in order to "grow" is not growth, it's relational anxiety and avoidance, and a denial of your actual relational needs.

The one-person psychological system is not psychologically or biologically productive. Men are not born driven away from a relational perspective, but due to gender trauma they are trained away from it. Women are trained to do most of the caregiving, and this is why they are more relationally focused. "It is important to remember that 'self' is a metaphor…built on a model of separation rather than connection… I believe that safety and psychological growth arise in good connection, not in the experience of self-sufficiency, autonomy" (Miller et al., 2004, p. 70). Most of our culture, and the majority of therapists, act as "boundary police," perpetuating the idea that fusion or moving from a self to a relational "us" is not healthy or safe.

Many myths dominate social and psychological discussions about sex and relationships. You need to unlearn the myths that bind you, as concepts such as codependence, moving too fast, and being too needy all ruin authentic and healthy drives and desires, in service of a made-up caricature of what is "healthy" and "acceptable." Relational and sexual health is not about adjustment to these fictions, but rather about confidence in one's own chosen path. In a culture that overvalues separation and distance, let's stop shaming those who have the capacity and confidence for early relational attachment. The problem with blind adherence to cultural dating and sex norms is that this is assimilation into whitewashed heteronormativity (or "phallicized whiteness," as critical theorists would say). Why is this bad? Because it is racist and sexist. It ignores all the many creative, healthy, fun, and brilliant ways of being and relating.

MARRIAGE'S NEW RULES

Marital-relationship rules and expectations need an update. The old rules were created out of rigid gender roles and inequalities. Traditional dating rules (often gender-based) are all manipulations and exploitative mind games, none of which are truly "relational." Adults ignore gender roles and dating games. Dating and relationships are about being authentic and vulnerable. Grow up and stop with the "men should…" and "women should…" The right time to text after a first date is whenever you want to, the right time to go on a second date is whenever you want to, and the right time to have sex with a new partner is whenever you want to.

Those with true relational esteem don't work to entrap another person into a relationship with them. If someone who is courting you uses ploys or games, or insists upon gender role expectations, RUN! This sexism and lack of relational maturity will manifest again and again, creating oppression and problems throughout the relationship.

The following are my ideas for new marital rules, as compared to the old rules and expectations.

1. Relationships are about fulfillment, happiness, and desire. *They are not about expectations.*
2. All partners have a commonality of roles. All partners have the same expectations. All partners raise children; all partners raise money. *Partners do not adhere to outdated gender roles and stereotypes.*
3. Either party can end or renegotiate the marital-relational contract. Marriage lasts until one partner is irreparably unhappy. *Marriage doesn't mean being held hostage because of an antiquated contract model.*
4. All partners balance the needs of the family with the needs of the self. *Partners do not need to be subservient to the needs of the family.*
5. Commitment comes from choice. *Commitment is not enforced by the marital contract* (Farrell, 1993, p. 45).

CHAPTER 7.

RELATIONAL SEX CRIMES

Culture and family can socialize you into believing there are specific "healthy" ways to run your relationships. There are many common marital-sexual-relational misconceptions and errors that frequently get played out within relationships. This chapter details several examples.

SECONDARY RELATIONSHIPS OR CHEATING

Healthy relationships are a natural balance of autonomy and partnership. This tension creates a struggle to both maintain a connection with someone and be single. Those who can't manage that tension often fall into secondary or tertiary relationships. Relationships go through many phases as individuals grow, age, and deal with new life events. As people and their needs change, relationships need to be renegotiated. When marriage partners aren't willing to discuss or explore newly developed needs, desires, or related shifts in boundaries, cheating usually occurs.

With the prevalence of online dating and readily available phone apps for casual sex, individuals can seek sexual outlets from their primary relationship with the swipe of a finger or the click of a mouse. These secondary relationships are intimacy blockers and safety valves for desires that the individuals want to explore but feel unable to ask of their primary partner.

SEX AS TRAUMA THERAPY

Nearly everyone who has had sex has also had traumatic and painful sexual experiences. Naturally the best way to heal these traumas is through healthy sex. Sex requires "allowing a place for trauma within sexuality…to maintain a place for shame and perversion within…discourses of sexuality rather than purging them of their messiness in order to make them acceptable" (Cvetkovich, 2003, p. 88).

Solo and partnered sex are both nurturing right-brain activities, like listening to music or doing yoga. Sex is the most powerful way to overcome personal and social body and sexual shame and stigma, as sexualizing oneself leads to increased self-worth.

PICK A PERVERSION

Traditionally, sexuality has been about the appropriate use of genitals in partnered sex, but many sexual pleasures do not involve the genital area, or even other people. Perversions, which have been given a bad name and are often misunderstood, encompass any pleasure-based act that deviates from heterosexual intercourse-based sexuality. We're not talking about acts that are illegal or dangerous—at least not all the time. Perversions are incredibly common; if you've ever had oral sex, anal sex, or sex with toys, you've engaged in perversions. Avoiding an expansive sexuality makes one that much likelier to develop psychological issues like erotophobia and sexual fear.

Diverse and creative sexual practices enhance and improve relationship and sexuality. Fetishes and perversions can build intimacy, communication, and closeness. Unless they cause objective and factual harm to a partner, fetishes are not deviant in nature but rather can be helpful to the sexual sustainability of relationships.

The theory of sex as a hardwired instinct that has reproduction as its sole goal has been challenged by modern studies of brain plasticity. The emergence of this research gives us another way to examine human sexuality. We live with ever-changing brains that are always evolving based on what we learn and experience. In this way, each sexual interaction creates new movement within our neurological system. We are constantly reshaping our brains based on our interactions. We do not require overt traumas to rewire our neurological systems. Sexuality is a powerful tool with which to transform ourselves when it is harnessed and redirected by the mind to form bonds and connection with others.

Fetishes and pornography can unlock early neurological networks formed during critical periods in adolescence. Pornography and other sexual novelty behaviors can form a new psychological network which wires all these together. This "killer combination" presses multiple sexual buttons at once, allowing for a higher level of arousal (Doidge, 2007, p. 111). The consequential rush of dopamine (pleasure neurotransmitters) can reinvigorate a dead sexual life. It's the neurological gift of novelty.

Perversions do not always involve objectification, but when they do, this can also enhance arousal and intimacy. Once we release sex from its stereotypical form, we can expand our definitions of arousal and sexuality.

Case Study: Dasa

Dasa had never had an orgasm with a partner. She had only dated heterosexual men, and although she "mostly" enjoyed sex with them, she was underwhelmed, disappointed, and getting bored. At twenty-six she was worried that if she hadn't really enjoyed sex yet, maybe it would never happen.

I wanted to learn more about the kind of sex she was having.

"I always have sex the regular way," she said. "My partners will make out with me, go down on me a bit, and then penetrate me vaginally. It feels good."

"Do they play with your clitoris?" I asked. "Most women need that to orgasm. Few are able to orgasm from vaginal penetration alone."

Yes, Dasa was aware of clitoral stimulation and typically asked her partners to play with her clit, or she played with it herself.

Next we discussed her sexual fantasies. What one fantasizes about, the type of pornography one watches, the kind of erotic writing one reads, the various sexual blogs, Tumblrs, and Instagram accounts one follows—these demonstrate the full erotic constellation that can reveal one's true sexual preferences. Dasa explained that she recently had started following a blog and Instagram account that featured stories and pictures of bondage sex play. She had been surprised to find that it aroused her.

I explained to Dasa that this could be what was missing from her sexuality. Adding creative and alternative sex play, which some people denigrate by labeling them "perversions," is a good way to amp up sexual arousal and keep sex fun. It's also a way to learn more about yourself and deepen intimacy with your partners.

Dasa spent some time on Tinder (a dating app) and found a couple that was interested in bondage. When they got together, the couple showed her how to experiment with bondage safely. Dasa reported back that this revived her interest in sex, and that she was now having regular orgasms, as well as learning that she had a sexual interest in women.

CENSORSHIP IS SEXPHOBIA

Society is experiencing a dramatic and catastrophic response to discussing and expressing sexuality. Most people don't realize that feeling anxiety is an important and necessary step in moving toward a healthier relationship with one's own sexuality.

Feeling uneasy about someone expressing their own sexuality isn't harmful or victimizing; it's a healthy sign of a need to increase one's tolerance level. The regulation of sexual language can lead to situations where sexual expression and confidence are shamed in the name of protection. Regulating such language boils down to an attempt to regulate sexuality. Sexphobic people can avoid living in the real world by silencing those whose comfort levels with sexuality make them uncomfortable. Sexuality does not equal sexism…the notion that individuals are inherently demeaned by sex and sexual expression reflects archaic, infantilizing stereotypes (Strossen, 2000). Most sexual censorship has the potential to be emotionally stunting and psychologically damaging, not protective.

While recognizing that words can be harmful, those uncomfortable with sex have used the concept of sexual harassment as a Trojan horse for smuggling their views on sexual expression into our law and culture. By influencing the legal and societal understandings of this concept, pro-censorship feminists have been alarmingly successful in effectively outlawing all sexual expression in many sectors of our society, even without any claim that the particular expression is subordinating or degrading (Strossen, 2000, p. 119).

This goes directly against the idea of sexual liberation and sexual health, where sex isn't treated as a "special" topic that needs to be policed and silenced. Flirting and courting, while sometimes seen as archaic and offensive, are really expressions of a "carnal recognition of an attractive stranger's appreciative gaze." Instead of fearing sex and your own sexual power, it would be healthier to make "finer distinctions between sexually inappropriate behavior and sexual harassment" (LeMoncheck & Hajdin, 1997, p. 28). The best outcome is that "in the absence of physical violence, sexual conduct cannot and must not be legislated from above, that all intrusion by authority figures into sex is totalitarian... The ultimate law of the sexual arena is personal responsibility" (Paglia, 1994, p. 23). Sex is not the enemy. The enemy is "the denial of female sexual agency" (Roiphe, 1994, p. 84).

Censorship is a symptom of anxiety. Sex education, psychotherapy, and frank and open public discourse are the right first steps to stop infantilizing our culture's approach to sexuality.

MONOGAMY IS ABOUT ANXIETY

A main driving force behind monogamy is the social control of sexual anxiety.

Monogamy essentially means that your partner owns your sexuality. This can work for many relationships if both partners have congruent sexual compatibility that allows for the various interest shifts of fantasies that life creates. However, many partners do not have the ability or interest to grow along with someone else's sexuality. For them, compulsory monogamy carries the possibility of devitalizing sex because sexual compatibility is missing. When a couple lacks sexual chemistry, "there is nothing as such about a monogamous sexual way of life that enhances, or makes more probable, its agent's flourishing" (Halwani, 2003, p. 74). Compulsory monogamy is what makes marriage problematic, not infidelity.

When one or both partners lose interest in sex, other options must be explored if they are going to remain together. If that doesn't happen, "monogamy becomes how the low-desire partner manages two anxieties at once: he forces the higher sexual desire to accept sex in accordance with his insecurities and immaturities, and he keeps his partner from seeking other partners she might prefer" (Schnarch, 2009, p. 141).

Early relational monogamy can be helpful as it increases the bonding and intimacy-building effects of sex. This provides a strong foundation for later attempts with other sexual-relational configurations, such as open relationships and bringing in other sexual partners. My psychological rule is: "*unhealthy* and *not solid* relationships that 'open up' become *unhealthy* and *not solid* open relationships. Whereas *healthy* and *solid* relationships that open become *healthy* and *solid* open relationships." If a closed monogamous relationship is not working, it's rare that opening it up will improve its health. Exploring non-monogamous relationships requires feeling safe and secure with your current partner, and adding others requires even more communication and relational work. If communication and empathy are already lacking, multiple partners won't be a functional solution.

I tell interested couples that a discussion about the possibility of opening up a relationship to multiple partners may need to be had many times over a long period of time before a decision is made, and the decision will also need to be discussed afterward to see if it was successful for both partners. No single way of sexually interacting with your partner is guaranteed to work throughout the life of a relationship, so both partners need to have flexible boundaries that change as needed. In times of distance and conflict, remaining monogamous can be best, because it keeps intention and focus on the primary relationship and partner's needs.

Monogamy is one sexual-relational choice, and as such should be selected only after partners have considered all other choices and decided which is best for them. Monogamy does create a brilliant crucible in which partners can be challenged to tolerate intimacy and realizations about one another. Relationships are cyclical and have different needs at different times. Decisions about monogamy are not permanent, but should be ongoing dialogues about how well it is working and whether to continue or try something else.

PROMISCUITY

Having many sexual experiences and partners leads to new ideas and ways of being. It also helps avoid consistency and boredom. Promiscuity can often bring life back into moribund sex lives while infusing creativity, novelty, and confidence into a relationship. Our sexual lives are the most powerful place to build our self-esteem and work through individual struggles, as most psychological issues are born from and healed within a relationship. Promiscuity allows for an openness to the world and enables multiple partners to see themselves as sexual subjects. This requires understanding your right and entitlement to all your sexual feelings, and the power to act on your sexual drives. Promiscuity allows you to practice assertive and direct sexual communication, and with the sexual experience gained, you build a comfort into your own sexual desires and limits.

Promiscuity can also lead to more closeness, more intimacy, and getting more from your relationships. Intimacy can be expressed in many ways, and even though sex is the most powerful and deepest, we over-rely on and over-prioritize romance and verbal communication to build intimacy. Sexual communication builds much stronger bonds, in particular psychological, physical/sexual, and social. Many see promiscuity as avoidance of intimacy, but in reality it's an integration of all levels of closeness and compatibility.

Gender myths abound about promiscuity, all of which attempt to limit an individual's ability to be sexual. The largest myth is that women can't have casual sex. Even those in the field of evolutionary psychology still support and perpetuate this falsehood. I call this sexual fascism. Any time a sexual fascist limits another's sexual behavior and abilities with stereotypes and prejudices due to their gender, not only are they oppressing someone's sexual possibilities and life, they are attempting to steal their freedom and happiness as a human being.

Women and men shouldn't tie themselves to these archaic ideas and norms. With the ever-too-slow dismantling of gender and gender roles, all people have the same capacities for sexual freedom, but these changes need to be constantly reinforced. Every time you call someone a slut, you are perpetuating the limits of her sexuality. Never allow someone to explain, limit, or challenge your sexual-relational behaviors or interests based on your gender. Promiscuity and casual sex are signs of sexual confidence. Healthy individuals do not hide behind or acknowledge gender in their decision-making. Using gender to explain someone's sexuality is naïve.

PORN IS "SAFETY"

Ideally, one day we'll have a fully sexualized society where all body types and shapes are accepted and equally eroticized. Once our Western culture gets over its incessant need to sexually shame people, porn will not be required. Until then, though, the safe sexual space that porn provides is absolutely necessary.

Being sexual is a good thing. Sexual arousal is a good thing. Watching pornography is a demonstration of sexuality. But linking sexual interest to self-worth is not a useful way to judge an individual's value or health. Those who detest porn do so because "it symbolizes everything they don't understand and can't control about their own bodies" (Paglia, 1994, p. 110).

Porn is often cited as a sexual vehicle for men, yet studies show that women consume porn in great numbers as well. "The search terms 'sex,' 'sex chat,' and 'sexy'...are equally as likely to be entered by women as they are by men... Women are more likely to type the search engine terms 'adult sex,' 'free sex,' and 'cyber sex' into the search engine than men are... Once free of the worry of who might see them doing it, women are indeed interested in sex and erotica" (Magnanti, 2013, p. 15). Porn is "another way to bring the erotic into our sex lives, in a way that women have historically been proscribed from doing" (Lynn, 2005, p. 80). Porn allows for imagination and possibility. Those whose sexuality has been shamed and marginalized—such as women, alternative sexual adventurers, or hypersexuals—need porn to rebuild self-worth and sexual health. The normalizing impact of seeing one's sexuality played out by others is enormously helpful for those who have sex that's considered perverted, deviant, etc.

The use of the pejorative label "porn," as opposed to erotica, demonstrates the dire need for further sexual enlightenment and education in our culture. Feminism, for instance, is often cited as being anti-pornography, but "most feminists do not see it as essentially more sexist than other parts of culture, such as great literature, advertising, or the bridal industry" (Gallop, 1997, p. 73). Phobias and miseducation about pornography run rampant, with both the media and psychology actively contributing to them. The issue to examine is not sexuality, but sexism. These two concepts are often confused. There are myriad books discussing how negative pornography is, written by "experts" who are in fact afraid of sexuality and incapable of discussing its worth. "Far from poisoning the mind, pornography shows the deepest truth about sexuality, stripped of romantic veneer. No one can claim to be an expert"—in psychology, sociology, medicine, gender, or philosophy (my words)—"who is uncomfortable with pornography, which focuses on our primal identity, our rude and crude animality. Porn dreams of eternal fires of desire, without fatigue, incapacity, aging, or death" (Paglia, 1994, p. 66).

Some of the terribly inaccurate "conventional wisdom" about porn includes: most kids leave porn behind when they grow up and form "real" relationships, avid porn use turns viewers into sexual predators, and masturbation and porn use are baser forms of sexuality. In actuality, these are all false. The majority of healthy adult men and women utilize some form of sexual materials during their own forms of solo sexuality, whether it be fantasizing, masturbating, reading erotica, or viewing sexual videos. It is one's personality, not one's porn consumption, that determines how a person will sexually relate to others. And individuals who masturbate and utilize pornography can also be in healthy relationships. One does not cancel out the other.

Healthy sex does not need to involve another individual. One of the most powerful components of masturbation is that you're doing it alone. This reinforces your own sexuality and frees you from thinking about your partner or partners.

Porn can also save lives. In studies of violent sex offenders and rapists (Diamond, 1999) perpetrators had often been exposed to minimal pornography and typically came from sexually repressive or religious upbringings. "As the use of porn increases, the rate of sex crimes goes down" (Diamond, 2009). Additionally, pornography usage has not been correlated with sexual victimization. "A decrease in the consumption of pornography was not correlated with a decrease in rape rates" (Kimmel & Linders 1996). D'Amato states, "those with the least access to the Internet showed an increase in rape of 53 percent. Studies of sex offenders (Gebhard, Gagnon, Pomeroy & Christenson 1965) found no significant differences in exposure to pornography in their histories when compared with that of non-sex offenders and controls" (2006, p. 4). Later research revealed similar findings; when the histories of convicted rapists were compared with a matched group of non–sex offenders, the conclusion was, "in reviewing the relation of aggression to sexual assault, it is time to discard the hypothesis that pornography contributes to increased sexual assault behavior and may actually provide a catharsis to alleviate sexual aggression" (C. E. Walker, 1970).

Statistically, cultures with more open sexual attitudes have fewer sex crimes. R. Green reported that "both rapists and child molesters use less pornography than a control group of 'normal' males" (1980, p. 68–97). Additional research shows that the most rigid (often religious) households produce more sexual predators. This also proves how fallacious is the argument that pornography makes men dangerous.

> Were we to ban words or images on the grounds that they had incited some susceptible individuals to commit crimes, the Bible would be in great jeopardy. No other work has more often been blamed for more heinous crimes by the perpetrators of such crimes. The Bible has been named as the instigating or justifying factor for many individual and mass crimes, ranging from the religious wars…to systemic child abuse and ritual murders. (Strossen, 2000, p. 258)

Of course, porn isn't without its downsides. Typically it does not accurately show the vast variability of sexual and anatomical functioning. As with all media, false representations are promoted and then internalized by the consumer. Porn promotes the idea that arousal comes easy and erections last as long as needed. The typical male erection will come and go, and cannot be expected to stay firm for the duration of all sexual activity. Couple this with media, especially television, that promote unrealistic romantic-sexual ideals, and you see the essential need to critically educate people about sexual expectations and abilities. If porn was viewed in a more socially acceptable light, it would create opportunities for a more diverse set of images and body types, making its positive aspects easier to see.

Representations of alternative bodies and identities as sexual and erotic are rare in our popular culture. One of the most treacherous ways to oppress and make a certain type of person invisible is to make them question their desirability. To counter this, I refer many clients to alternative kinds of pornography so that they can see various body types and body parts eroticized to build sexual and body esteem. Porn can increase one's identification as a sexual person and body. Non-normative pornography and imagery can "give viewers the opportunity to recognize, re-imagine, and acknowledge that being out of line, being crooked, being different and being variant can be smoking hot" (Erickson, 2012, p. 326). It's important for individuals to find erotic imagery that gives them the experience of seeing their own self eroticized.

The benefits of porn highly outweigh the negatives, so long as it is viewed with a critical eye. "Sexually explicit materials may well be the only source of sexual information or pleasure for many people who, for a host of reasons, do not have sexual contact with others—shy or inhibited people, people with mental or physical disabilities, people with emotional problems... people who are quite young or old, geographically isolated people" (Strossen, 2000, p. 164). Porn is an essential part of the battle against sexual normativity and regulation. It allows us to unlearn and undo the socialization and internalization of dominant norms about which types of bodies have permission to be sexual. Our arousal constellation is built from the images we consume. Porn is an overt and direct way to work with the plasticity of our sexuality. It does not need more restrictions; it needs more diverse bodies, styles, and behaviors.

CHILDREN GROW SIDEWAYS

Children are born with a fully functioning sexual response system. "The process of shaping a child's sexuality begins from day one" (Ehrenberg & Ehrenberg, 1988, p. 28). We have created a conceptual deprivation chamber called "childhood" to protect ourselves from acknowledging that children have a sexuality long before they enter the state of "adulthood," which is an arbitrary designation that differs country by country and culture by culture. The child—much like the disabled, the psychologically disordered, and the sexually diverse—has a policed body that creates fear for the dominant and normative culture.

The mandates given to children to limit exploration of their burgeoning sexuality are ways of training them to not have confidence in their internal experiences and to keep them infantilized. The adolescent experience, especially when paired with schooling, is closely tied to a child's burgeoning sexuality. "Early childhood, not puberty…is the first critical period for sexuality" (Doidge, 2007, p. 98). Children arrive with no awareness of sexual boundaries or understanding of what constitutes an acceptable target for arousal and pleasure.

Sexual knowledge is not dangerous. We must let go of the need to repress reality so as to maintain the obsession with "innocence" that we falsely connect with the introduction of sexuality. "The most damaging abuse of power comes from well-intentioned adult efforts to control children's sexual knowledge" (Hubbard & Verstraete, 2013, p. xx). Sexuality is not damaging. What drives abstinence-only sex education is really a futile attempt to thwart children's ability to mature. "Teen sex is a normative phase of aging" (Schalet, 2011, p. 3). Children have sexual rights and deserve privacy. Adult interference in a child's healthy sexual development typically creates more problems than it solves.

Adult involvement is also often mostly about reducing their own anxiety. Remember, problematic behavior is about a lack of impulse control, boundaries, and empathy, not about diverse sexual interests. Children need to develop sexual confidence.

> We can look at a girl's sexual talk and games and call her prematurely slutty or, using a more clinical word, over-sexualized. We can look at her plans to play sexually with another girl, the sexual feelings she has with another girl, and we might

> call her lesbian. Or we might simply say, "this is what children do, they have bodies, they have sexual feelings; the exploration and expression of both are *normal*" no matter whom they are with. (Lamb, 2001, p. 3)

Adult dysfunctions are a result of seeing the body and its eroticism as shameful and dirty. This is often learned in childhood. "Sexual clinics treat sexual dysfunctions, but only parents can prevent them" (Yates, 1982, p. 131). What can a parent do to raise a sexually healthy child?

1. Be comfortable with their own sexuality
2. Give children a balanced perspective on sex (neither over- or under-emphasizing it)
3. Treat eroticism like all other important developmental aspects: with respect and honest discussion
4. Encourage their child's sexual independence
5. Provide good examples by which to model intimacy (Yates, 1982)

VIRGINITY

Sexual discovery should be celebrated because it is a movement into an experience of deeper intimacy and pleasure with oneself or another. It allows for a new space of exploration and growth. The concept of praising holding on to one's virginity or, worse, asexuality, damages both the body and the psyche. It polices boundaries by arbitrarily defining what "real sex" is. The phrase "losing one's virginity" implies that one can cross over from a space of integrity (being a virgin) into a space of degradation. It's not healthy to perpetuate the message that an individual's worth comes solely from use of his or her body or sexuality.

SEX/LOVE ADDICTION OR JUST TYPICAL LIFE

Modern clinical and social terms like "sex addiction" and "love addiction" are highly misused and misunderstood, even by mental health professionals. These syndromes are strongly individualistic and are erroneously applied to nontraditional styles. They are a moral ideology on steroids.

Our culture's obsession with labeling strongly expressed sexualities "sex addiction" creates a society devoid of any colorful and non-typical sexual expression. It also removes the "offending" individual's sexual arousal and creative sexual desires, leaving behind the stain of moral stigma. "The ideal model presented for sexually addicted women is a social purity vision of a spiritually based, monogamous sexuality that is always relationally oriented. Any variation of this is pathologized" (Irvine, 2005, p. 329).

Sex addiction research and literature is bloated with attempts to split sexuality and arousal into notions of good versus bad. This separation shames part of one's arousal and sexual orientation, creating an intrapsychic split that causes a healthy part of one's sex drive to be viewed as a negative. Healthy sexuality and sexual functioning require an integration between your orientation and what arouses you, without shame entering the mix.

Most sexual addiction treatments view repetition or compulsion as an unhealthy drive to be tamed, contained, and clinically treated. This noxious clinical lens impedes the success and sustained pleasure of accepting one's own sexuality. This has created a highly lucrative industry as specialists falsely pathologize and label clients with shame-based identities that create havoc in both their social and sexual lives. I warn individuals about accepting a clinical diagnosis of sex addiction, as it can have a serious impact on their sexuality and relationships. All diagnostic labels, syndromes, and disorders are essentially conceptual, theoretical, arbitrary, political in nature, and based on cultural norms that are incapable of being applied to every individual. These diagnoses are a form of social control.

All mental health struggles exist on a continuum between healthy and problematic behaviors. Each of us falls closer to one end of the scale or the other. Many sexual "illnesses" are in fact cultural outcomes that are erroneously being diagnosed as disorders, thereby ignoring their social and cultural creation and maintenance. Currently the mental health field carries "the imposition of a biomedical paradigm over social events or problems," which means "a reliance on individual treatment solutions" and not directing clinicians to "end the double standard, improve sex education, or expose destructive and coercive sexual ideologies" (Irvine, 2005, p. 330).

The final and most essential flaw with diagnosing "sex addiction" is that the "experts" are working and speaking outside of their scope of competence and education. Their lack of training in human sexuality, sex therapy, and clinical sexology make these practitioners woefully ignorant at best and potentially dangerous at worst. They work with an almost pathological aversion and antipathy to anything that is sexually and relationally non-normative.

Case Study: Rich

Rich was dragged into therapy by his partner. She explained that Rich was a sex addict who looked at porn every day. She felt this was disgusting and considered it cheating. This scenario is not rare, as few understand the healthy uses of pornography and masturbation.

I asked Rich how he felt about his sexuality. "I'm happy and have no concerns about my masturbation, but I'm unsure because it makes my partner so upset."

I like to hear that all people masturbate, because solo sex is a fun part of our sexuality, comes under only our control, and is separate from our partnered relationship. However, the issue here was not the masturbation but how these two dealt with sex together as a couple. I explained that any "couple issues" needed to be dealt with as a team.

A partner can share how someone's masturbation impacts her but, married or not, she has no right to exert control over it. Masturbating daily is quite healthy, as is using pornography, so I explained to Rich's partner that he wasn't a sex addict. Even when monogamy has been chosen, as with Rich and his partner, one cannot try to control the solo aspects of one's partner's sexuality.

Rich's partner wasn't convinced. "He has had hundreds of sex partners. Clearly that's an addiction to sex."

"Wrong again," I said. Addiction isn't about quantity but rather the consequences of a behavior and how much control one has over it. Sex cannot be addictive, I explained, because it's a drive that is always active within most of us. Much like we cannot become food or sleep addicts but we can struggle with regulation of our eating and sleeping, some find it a struggle not to be sexually compulsive. I asked Rich's partner what made her so anxious about sex. Why was she so scared by Rich's full and active sex life, prior to meeting her and now as well?

It turned out that Rich and his partner had different sex drives, templates for healthy sex, and sexual histories. As with most couples, they needed to do significant work to understand one another's differences.

Many partners want to punish others based on their prior sex lives. This is never acceptable. Sexual development includes exploration with different partners and different behaviors. Never apologize for your sexual history. More importantly, don't share your sexual history unless your partner is sexually mature enough to hear it. Some of those who have been erroneously diagnosed and forced into "sex addiction treatment" are told differently. They are told that disclosing their sexual history creates trust, when in fact it often creates an irreconcilable tension if one partner believes the other owns their sexuality and does not allow privacy and healthy boundaries. This is why it's crucial to seek diagnosis and treatment from a certified sex therapist.

CHAPTER 8.

THE MYTH OF SEXUAL DYSFUNCTIONS

DIAGNOSES AS ATTEMPT TO POLICE

Sexual dysfunctions don't exist. These diagnoses are attempts to pathologize diversity and standardize sexual functioning. Most issues are due to social reactions and misunderstandings and not the actual sex. The narrative of individuals with sexual-relational disorders should not be one about dysfunction and pathology, but instead about miseducation, stigma, and social shaming. There is no "normal"; normal is *not* the goal. From birth, culture, family, and media do their best to hold this "normal" as the template for healthy functioning.

Each individual will operate differently sexually, with variations and issues to be expected. We will all have problems with our sexuality at points in our lives. This is sexuality, not pathology. Most sexual dysfunctions are not due to disorder or the failure of some part of the body but are failures to perform sex in a way that is socially acceptable or desirable.

All dysfunctions and mental disorders have a health component to them (i.e., depression is positive and leads to more focus, schizophrenia is related to creativity). Sexual "disorders" are deemed so due to prejudice and oppression. They are diagnosed from a heterosexual, intercourse-focused, genital-obsessed matrix. For example: a woman whose vagina tightens and rejects a penis is told she has "vaginismus" because the assumption is she should *want* a penis; it is seen as a requirement for health. But if her mouth rejects fellatio by gagging, no disorder is assigned. This is because penis-in-vagina hetero intercourse sex is prioritized over all other forms of sex. If sex were understood to not require ejaculation to end, then delayed ejaculation would not exist either. The constructed "disorder" of premature ejaculation is similar in that it only has significance because sex cannot continue after a man ejaculates, in a model wherein intercourse is the only correct form of sex. These heterosexual sex–based problems only exist because the genitals are seen as primary organs for sex. The true issue is with the psycho-medical field's obsessive-compulsive disorder around intercourse. *That* is what needs treatment and therapy.

These non-disordered "disorders" and faux dysfunctions are pathogenic medicine that paralyzes individuality and diversity with "a belief that impairment or disability…is inherently negative and, should the opportunity present itself, ought to be ameliorated, cured or indeed eliminated" (Campbell, 2009, p. 5). This suffocates sexual variation and sexual autonomy. The problem is the paradigm, not the genitals. When sex doesn't go the way you want or think it should, it's a chance for you to deal with the disappointment of your fantasy and focus on humanity and reality. This is when sex helps us grow up (or, as I like to say, "grow sideways"). Growing sideways means growing away from expectations and norms. It's a conscious attempt to bypass the shaming and mythic hierarchy of what's deemed healthy and mature versus unhealthy and immature, and instead move toward a radically authentic path of your own subjective needs and wants.

Whose penis/clitoris/vagina is this? Your partner, medicine, psychology, and religion all claim ownership. The "sex addict" is a constellation of socio-sexual-relational factors that combine to produce and then police a "disorder" that becomes colonized by diagnoses. The psychological work is to free yourself and escape the power being exerted upon your body and your pleasure. There is no dysfunctional sex or body type, but instead there are people who are sexually diverse or sexually atypical. The disordering of anatomy is an abuse of sexuality. Sexual disorders are the outcome of all that is sexually and relationally wrong with our culture. It forgets that pleasure is the only part of sex that counts!

FREUD RUINED US

Freud theorized that to reach "adult health," one must relinquish "pleasure in non-genital zones, focus on penis and vagina, and achieve the correct and healthy aim of sex-discharge from penis into vagina" (Dimen, 2003, p. 44). This theory of "health" probably singlehandedly made us all neurotic about what is considered sexually healthy, and created all sexual disorders, including the idea of distinct female and male sexuality and the idea that mature adult sex must be penetrative genital intercourse only.

Without the proliferation of the aforementioned perspective of health, and the dissemination of all the psychosexual literature born from it, my clinical practice would not need to exist. The concept of penetration as sex, with genitals as the tools, has vandalized the sexuality of all individuals, and the concepts of distinct female and male sexualities is a dualist perspective ignoring the true multiplicities of gender and sexuality. We determine which body parts are sexual by social definition and socialization, and we prioritize specific procreative-based anatomy as sexual parts while illegitimizing the rest of body.

When pleasure, and not procreation, is the main goal of sex, the genitals are irrelevant, as erections and vaginal penetration are not required. We are in a post-genital phase and must move the focus to other body parts. Sexual dysfunctions are all hetero, procreative, and genital centric. If you are not having sex only to create a child, or are not heterosexual, then non-insertion, non-genital sex become more relevant and the rest of the body can be explored sexually. This allows for anal, clitoral, and oral sex (among many others) as legitimate and necessary forms of sex. It also mitigates fears of teen pregnancy.

Penetration is oppressive, and deprioritizing penetration is crucial, partly because vaginal penetration is often about male pleasure. The majority of women require or at least prefer clitoral stimulation, rendering vaginal penetration secondary or tertiary to their pleasure.

HISTORICAL SEX SHAMING

As cultural beliefs change, many formerly held theories are exposed as groundless. This is evidenced by psychology and psychiatry's legacy of sexual abuse with a past list of fictitious "disorders" such as gender identity disorders, homosexuality, masturbation, nymphomania, Freudian penis envy, non-vaginal penetrative sex, and non-procreative sex, and the current sex-hating diagnoses such as sex and love addiction. These sexual diagnoses "have all been exposed as nothing more than psychotherapeutic labels for culturally held prejudices" (Watters & Ofshe, 1999, p. 40). They are not benign designations but powerful classifications that have "huge societal significance and determine all sorts of important things that have an enormous impact on people's lives—like who is considered well and who is sick; what treatment is offered; who pays for it; who gets disability benefits…who gets to be hired for a job, can adopt a child, or pilot a plane, or qualifies for life insurance…and much more" (Frances, 2013, p. xii).

The *DSM* as a diagnostic manual has the role of "regulating the boundaries of normality" (Warner & Wilkins, 2003, p. 169). So its continued usage, legitimization of, and reliance upon sexual disorders is medical malpractice and sexual abuse. These diagnoses are not used in my clinical practice, nor would they belong in another competent practitioner's office.

SEXUAL DISORDER AS HEALTHY FUNCTIONING

The concept of sexual dysfunction is another attempt to normalize and shame common sexual experiences and frame them as abnormalities. "The diagnosis is everything…it's a sentence that the condemned person spends the rest of a lifetime living with" (Farber, 2012, p. xi). Individuals are made into subjects, and the labels and diagnoses become attempts at surveillance to bring them closer to a norm. "Truth" is both disciplinary and marginalizing. Psychology, and along with it sexology and sex and relational therapy, are being co-opted and usurped by medicine and the medical model.

Diagnoses often take sexual behaviors and transform them from temporary aberrations that might be ameliorated via insight, change, or therapy into the specification of types of individuals. "The role of modern medicine was not to transform human capacities but to restore a lost normativity" (N. Rose, 2007, p. 81). This statement beautifully exemplifies all that is wrong with psychology as currently practiced. It works to restore "normativity," but *whose* normativity? Most likely that of older, white, higher socioeconomic, archaic-modeled mental health "experts" who have rendered their thoughts useless because they live and think outside the current paradigm of sexual-relational culture.

This leads us to my clinical mantra: "normal is *not* the goal," especially since there is no measure by which to judge and evaluate "normal." We are in a post-biology, post-nature epoch, and as such need to create new visions and models for living. Sexual-relational life should remain the domain of sexologists, sociologists, and philosophers.

SEX PROBLEMS ARE COMMON

Sexual dysfunctions do not exist. They are only a result of unrealistic expectations. For example, with erectile dysfunction, the "misleading term implies that these men have a problem in their penises, but the problem is in their heads" (Doidge, 2007, p. 105). There is no "right" way for sexuality to function or operate. Diversity is part of humanity and life. The medical field has hijacked sexuality and forced it into boxes of good versus bad, ignoring the many relational and psychological factors that create, sustain, and extinguish sexual arousal and functioning.

Most medical therapies for sexual "issues" are anti-sex and anti-relational, and they shame healthy cycles of sexual functioning, arousal, desire, and orgasm. They ignore diversity and pleasure and only examine functionality. Often they reinforce conformity to an ideal that ignores the benefits of sexual variance. Sex is about far more than just how firm a penis can be, the length of time it can stay that way, and how well a vagina accepts its insertion. A surgery or pill to solve this "problem" ignores couples' issues, sexual interests, and intrapersonal struggles.

Many sex therapists are also arbitrators of "intercourse therapy," making penetration and penile functionality the sole purpose of sex and sexual health. And at the clinical bottom are sex addiction therapists, who lack sex training and work from an addiction model, shaming many healthy parts of sexuality and utilizing traumatizing tools like polygraphs and disclosures.

Sexual problems are normal and should be expected. Sexual "disabilities" and "issues" are not the sign of failure that we have come to see them as. Bordo states, "the penis is not a dildo" (1999, p. 64), recognizing that it is a live, fragile, complex organ, run by a live, fragile, complex system, attached to a live, fragile, complex human being. It is not just a biology of hydraulics, as urologists and dispensers of Viagra want us to believe. It carries relational, intrapsychic, cultural, and familial symbolism.

At some point in our lives, everyone will have suffered through a few sexual troubles. Individuals should see difficulties in functioning not as problems but as challenges to expand their understanding of how to be sexual, including experimenting with behaviors and instruments they have never tried. When an issue occurs during sex, it should be worked around. If a penis goes flaccid, you still have fingers and a tongue. Intercourse, sexuality, and pleasure do not require genitals. The average American time of thrusting with an erection after penetration is two and a half minutes (Dodson, 1996, p. 16). It takes most women far longer than that to get fully aroused and reach orgasm.

In addition, one should look at whom one is trying to be sexual with. A woman's low sexual desire, which is currently diagnosable as a disorder, could be nothing more than a healthy response to the fact that she's dating an asshole. If you don't respect a person, you most likely won't want to be sexual with them. If your low interest in sex were to be "treated" with medication, that would ignore a healthy part of yourself that is seeking safety. Likewise, if your wife isn't the most pleasant woman to communicate with, of course you're not going to want to have sex with her.

Nonetheless, pharmaceutical companies and doctors have turned natural variations in sexual functioning into a biological problem to fix, either with new medication or with flawed theories. "The drugs either try to increase vaginal blood flow (implied: women don't get turned on easily, so drug intervention is needed), or they try to boost testosterone (implied: women don't have hormones like men's, so drug intervention is needed). Others focus on neurotransmitters (implied: there's something lacking in women's brain chemistry, so drug intervention is needed)" (Magnanti, 2013, p. 22). All of these failed theories show that there is no actual medical problem to fix.

Rebuffing definition and category allows you to be all your many selves, which are all always changing depending upon your current relationships and your place in culture and history. You are not bound by who you were in past relationships, which is something many diagnoses can lead you to believe. Individuals are better served by being led *out* of a category or diagnosis versus being walked into one. This misdirection is one of traditional psychotherapy and psychiatry's greatest flaws.

BASTARDIZATION OF SEX BY MEDICINE

Sexual disorders are socially created based on hegemonic norms, and they bring huge monetary gains to the medical establishment with its various functioning-only-focused treatments. All the current medicinal strategies completely ignore the purpose of sex by vandalizing the concept of pleasure in service of "correct" biological operating. For example, there is no "healthy" length of time for an erection to last, but Viagra reinforces this mythical problem by maintaining the anxiety and focus on penis performance.

Sexual treatments, diagnoses, and therapeutic forms of practice may be attempts to rehabilitate or heal wounded or problematic sex, but they "also invent new regimes for controlling and regulating the sexuality we think we are affirming" (Bruhm & Hurley, 2004, p. x). Many disorders, like intimacy disorders, are really just value differences. This "performance script is stoutly reinforced by the *DSM* used by health professionals who treat sexual problems. In this *DSM*, the criteria for sexual dysfunction are all physical, and they all relate specifically to problems with intercourse" (Ogden, 2008, p. 24).

Low sexual desire is relative and it's to be expected, as no two people have the same desire level. Managing this is a couples issue and not a hormonal one to be solved with a patch or pill. In the *DSM*, "desire disorder" doesn't refer to erotic feelings or interest in sexual relationships. "It only means a lack of interest in the act of penis-vagina intercourse" (Ogden, 2008, p. 24).

This definition is clearly heteronormative and reduces sex to just vaginal penetration, ignoring anal sex, oral sex, and a wealth of other pleasure-based activities. The prioritizing of vaginal sex has no basis and invalidates the health of all other forms of sex. *All* forms of sexuality are appropriate and legitimate.

We live in a society of untrained human-sexuality "experts" determining the standards we then attempt to live up to. These norms are statistical, meaning that there are many people falling on either side of the averages. Sexual reality is one of complete irregularity. The sexual disorders in the *DSM* are based upon arbitrary expectations, with social politics guiding the manual's every move. People are segregated into diagnoses that deplete their self-esteem by forcing them into a vilified social category or identity based on junk science that amounts to nothing more than random boundaries between "healthy" and "unhealthy." The source of the problem is not seen as relevant to the diagnosis-based solution, thereby bypassing the real intrapersonal and interpersonal work. Our cultural anxieties leave us feeling powerless without the intervention of medicine.

Human sexuality and sex therapy should be kept within the hands of those who have been appropriately trained and certified as sex therapists. Sexuality is loaded and laden with our history (trauma, successes, failures), our self-esteem, our family/social/religious messaging, etc. There cannot and should not be any expectations for sex other than pleasure and self-enhancement.

The Freudian days of classifying some forms of sex as mature and others as immature are, thankfully, behind us—but not far enough. Too many mental health professionals and "experts" relegate sexual behavior that is not vanilla to erroneous, nonexistent, and shaming categories. Some of these include:

- "Trauma repetition" is the idea that sexual behaviors that are not "traditional" are the result of a past trauma that is being reenacted in the present, and therefore unhealthy—yet every single thing we do is born out of attempts to cope with our history of small and big traumas, our attempts to mitigate the use of historically needed coping mechanisms, and our ability to deal with triggers and work on not reliving past experiences in the present.

- "Acting out"—but that's what humans do: we often engage in behaviors that communicate what we cannot or will not put into words. Yet often a healthy sex drive will be shamed into being seen as "acting out," as opposed to being seen as necessary functioning and interest.
- "Intimacy disordered"—this bullshit disorder is truly subjectively used. There is no standard for "healthy intimacy," as every person has different levels of interest. Typically the higher-desiring partner will use his or her level to determine where his or her partner should be as well. In addition, every culture has its own norm, so what is "healthy" in America may be seen as antisocial, obnoxious, and boundaryless in Switzerland.
- "Pathological"—most of sexuality seems to find its way into this trash-can label by psychologists. Yet for there to be a pathology, there must be a standard of health against which to compare it. Sex is not about pathogens, so such labels implying so must be seen as institutional attempts to control and normalize. Sex is about how it feels, not how long an erection lasts, how wet one gets, or how often a couple has sex.

Sex can be procreative, recreational, or relational. Only procreation has the definitive need for intercourse, penetration, and (male) orgasm. Most sex is for fun, pleasure, and bonding, and as such it does not require anything to be average, specific, or functional.

NO HIERARCHY

A sexual-relational (psychosexual) theory that focuses on diversity ignores the tyranny of living in the shadows of statistical averages and central tendencies. Most sexual developmental theories attempt to critique behavior utilizing a standardized model of fixed averages and expectations. But no sex, sexual behavior, or sexuality should be considered inherently better, more legitimate, or healthier than another.

IN SEARCH OF THE "PERFECT PENIS"

We have sexual pioneers like Masters and Johnson to thank for creating a flawed sense of sex that we are still trying to dispel. They said "normal, healthy, proper sexuality means that the vagina works properly (opening nicely and getting wet when it's supposed to), the penis works properly (getting hard and ejaculating at the proper time) and the orgasm works properly" (Tiefer, 1997, p. 107). This view treats bodies as machines, ignoring all pleasure and desire.

A performance-based sexual model creates problems, failures, and dysfunctions. A pleasure-based model—the actual goal of sex—has no space for such constructs.

Urologists work to keep themselves in business by framing most issues as biological and ignoring context, relationship, and the reality that penile functioning is complex. A "disordered" penis often operates fine by not getting erect in situations within which one should not be sexual, such as when there is lack of interest, relational conflict, exhaustion, or boredom.

The sexual-medical pharma complex is always working to create new "needs," also framing erectile issues as solely biologically driven.

The self-help industry is well intentioned, but led by

untrained sexologists who all speak from the same sexphobic and relationally anxious place. Far too many sexual-relational twelve-step cases in my office complain that they are now suffering from sexual anorexia and the effects of shaming of sexual preferences such as the use of sex workers, non-relational sex, and masturbation with porn.

Insurance companies favor dispensing pills to augment psychological treatment. These medications give men robust erections but leave them in toxic relationships that include sex that is not worth being erect for in the first place.

Why is all this problematic? It ignores partnership, pleasure, and the rest of the erogenous body. It leaves sex as exclusively biologically driven, hetero-exclusive, and intercourse-based only. Any shift from this becomes viewed as a sexual disorder.

SEXUAL DIAGNOSES BYPASS REAL ISSUES

Any treatment, program, or theory that does not address or dismantle the systemic and regulatory damage from social-psychological institutional oppression and "norms" is psychological bypassing and a superficial Band-Aid. This is what keeps individuals trapped in toxic perspectives and systems, being shamed for healthy, self-directed attempts at freedom. These anti-client interventions blame and victimize individuals with diagnoses like "sex addict" instead of dismantling the system of monogamy, which is the real issue and problem.

For example, low sexual desire is an expected stage of any relationship, and not a disorder. After the early days of a relationship, a natural tension of wanting both pair bonding and sexual freedom arises in most individuals. The lack of desire for sex with a current long-term partner is not a disorder. This is called "victim blaming," putting responsibility on an individual for something outside their control. It's a systemic issue that habituation occurs and excitement, interest, and arousal decrease. Providing clients with new skills merely reinforces the powerlessness they feel over the lack of novelty in their sexual life, and it doesn't address the issues that arise from monogamy. This type of issue is a typical consequence of choosing a monogamous, sexually committed relational style in the long term. Current treatments attempt to push back against and ignore the expected trajectory of sexual-relational functioning, instead shaming partners for their lack of interest and further reinforcing the flawed idea that sex can or should occur at the same rate for the duration of all relationships. This is where the sexology and psychology fields demonstrate their fears of challenging marriage and monogamy. They prescribe flimsy exercises to try to induce novelty, but these ultimately produce watered-down sex that is generally not worth having, and therefore they fail. The individuals then feel shamed and disordered, as opposed to being empowered by the understanding that long-term sexual desire at the same rate for the same partner is a near impossibility. Other sexual-relational options need to be discussed and introduced.

Why must one want to be sexual? What about asexuality? "Compulsory sexuality" must not be essentialized or reified. Sexual and relational health and fitness demand the freedom to choose the style and internal process and structure of one's romantic-sexual relationships. The desire to be sexually promiscuous means having all the sex one wants *and does not want* as well. It's okay to not want to be sexual.

What level of desire should one have? There will *always* be a partner with less desire, and one should never be diagnosed as "disordered" because of this. Sex is not a machine or under the jurisdiction of your partner's requests. Our health should be based on others' subjective needs, not diagnosed in reflection and reaction to our partner (and therefore changing with each new partner) or by our sexphobic and norm-obsessed culture.

Each subculture has its own norms anyway, and I know I would not want my health based upon the behavior of those I do not identify with.

Then there's premature ejaculation. How long should one last? Who says? Based on what? In many European countries, ejaculating quickly is a sign of true arousal and attraction to your partner, but in American it is seen as a flaw, which is a sign of the cultural influence and lack of true objectivity to the diagnosis. What is an "erectile issue"? You get erect when you get erect. Instead of focusing solely on ejaculation as the terminus to sex, people should use "circular sexuality": having sex that starts and ends with whatever it starts and ends with. Sex is not about getting to/ending with penetration/intercourse, so if an erection/ejaculation happens before you want it to, move on to other pleasure/connective/bonding/relational activities.

The "treatment" in these cases ought to be psychological, not pharmaceutical, to find out why one partner is putting pressure on the other's penis, why she doesn't feel attractive if he loses his erection, why he is forcing her to be more sexual or intercourse based, and why these are even issues. Most men are relieved when I tell them there is no issue with their penis, and to tell their partners that they need to be less penis/penetration focused. These men need to have higher self-esteem and not take the behavior of an unconscious penis personally.

The definition of health must be challenged to reflect current truths, rather than continuing to hold people accountable to erroneous, oppressive, archaic data.

DEATH OF THE VAGINA AND PENIS

Once sex is liberated from procreation, the notion of sexual organs as exclusively reproductive organs becomes irrelevant. The vagina and penis are no longer needed for sex. The notion of "sexual dysfunction" meaning a body part that does not function procreatively can be dismissed. Sex is bifurcated from reproductive therefore sex is no longer required. Reproduction can occur in non-partnered and asexual ways, such as artificial insemination. Sexual dysfunctions only exist in an uneducated and sexually unsophisticated time period.

The current utopian concept of the "penis" is no longer a sustainable or realistic one. What was once a body part is now a theoretical cyborg and piece of machinery. "A cyborg is a cybernetic organism, a hybrid of machine and organism, a creature of social reality as well as a creature of fiction" (Haraway, 1991, p. 149). With the aid of technology, medication, and urology, we have journeyed from penis to posthuman cyborg "phallus." We have not been able to tolerate that the penis is a flawed, complex, and fragile piece of anatomy, so from this anxiety of a failed utopian penis emerges the medically enhanced posthuman phallus. Our culture carries with it, especially medically and therapeutically, an impulse to "normalize" (normalcy equaling ablebodiedness) and standardize everything.

We must return to more realistic expectations. The penile functioning "clock" for erectile and ejaculatory time has been quantified subjectively by individuals and medicine—both arbitrarily—and with posthuman methods we now have the option of a cyborg phallus that rejects natural biological individuality and, with a commodified capitalist perspective, operates at will regardless of arousal, desire, sexual context, environment, or partner choice. This rides on the back of compulsory heterosexuality with its compulsory ablebodiedness. The vision of the "correct" penis is prioritized over relationship and pleasure. This is heteronormativity and patriarchy at their most oppressive. The obsessive focus upon traditional intercourse practices is erotophobia. Timing is used to normalize and pathologize, leaving no space for reality or diversity. Sexual health and sexual freedom both require a comfort with alternative temporalities, which are actually typical temporalities, as no one lives in a way that is fully aligned with the trajectory of "normal" or "standard."

MARGINAL EQUALS PERVERT

The brilliance of the "queering" of life and related "queer practices" is that it challenges conventional expectations. It enhances the possibility of non-normativity with an alternative trajectory and allows new sexual-relational visions to be healthy and acceptable. Once we do away with the medical model and its toxic spawn the *DSM*, sex becomes liberated and individuals can reach new desires. The future of sex outside the nexus and orbit of diagnostic labels allows for new visions and truths. It is actually much healthier to live outside the confines of the medical model, away from binaries like order versus disorder, functional versus dysfunctional, and healthy versus pathological. The sex addiction world always provides clear examples of flawed reasoning directed toward shaming non-normative and non-couple-centric sexual-relational styles. Our Western culture is obsessed with a heterocentric vertical trajectory of growing up. Stockton discusses "growing sideways" as an alternative to the traditional vertical movement "toward marriage, work, and reproduction" (2009, p. 4)

CHAPTER 9.

NO IDENTITY, GENDER, OR SEXUAL ORIENTATION

We should strive to have no identity, gender, or sexual orientation, because a coherent identity is impossible. Identity is far too unstable, multiple, fluid, and contradictory. Labels around sex and identity are limiting and do not allow for the flexibility that sexual health and relational sustainability require. Language constructs our psychology and our self-representation.

Labels like these create a binary, with exclusions, privilege, and limits. That in turn breeds a hierarchy where one end of the binary is seen as more desirable or acceptable than its opposite. For the concept of "female" to exist, there needs to be "male," and this false dichotomy also creates a nonexistent difference in types of individuals.

The idea of "universal sex temperaments" is nothing more than male and female stereotypes. "A girl's sexuality is conceptualized as quiescent and inert, but also deeply fragile…in contrast, masculine heterosexuality is present, active, and natural" (Egan, 2013, p. 61). And yet all these widely accepted views are both wrong and limiting because "girls, like boys, are deeply sexual, and deeply aggressive creatures" (Lamb, 2001, p. 9). The danger in these erroneous gender diagnoses is that they lead to slut-shaming and psychic violence for those whose sexuality falls outside this codified behavioral binary.

> Despite the evident belief of many that masculinity and femininity are unchanging and inevitable properties of male and female bodies, respectively,

> these attributes are in fact culturally specific and historically conditioned. If this were not so, men and women could be expected to behave identically everywhere, in all cultures and at all times; but this is not the case, as much historical, anthropological, and sociological research indicates. (Buchbinder, 2013, p. 4)

The field of developmental psychology has been an integral part of perpetuating misunderstandings around healthy identity development. At a time when little was known (or allowed) about the diversity of gender, and fear existed about non-normativity, a flawed identity trajectory was constructed to define "healthy" lines of identity formation and development. This is still used to train individuals in the ways of being a boy or a girl, depending on their gender diagnosis. "This unfolding drama is predicated on a model of men, women, and babies as the universal family type, which we know no longer to be true, and posits that all children have three developmental gender tasks: (1) establishing a core gender identity as either male or female…(2) learning what it means to be male or female and learning that it is a permanent fixture of who they are…and (3) establishing their sexual orientation" (Ehrensaft, 2011, p. 25). None of these three tasks are correct or needed, but they are still used to diagnose healthy people as gender dysphoric by poorly trained therapists, confused and anxious parents, and those in the non-sexology-educated medical field.

Labels create "-isms," all of which cause problems:

- sexism: one gender is seen as more legitimate than another
- heterosexism: heterosexuality is seen as more legitimate or healthier than homo- or bisexuality
- monosexism: people who are exclusively attracted to members of a single sex or gender are viewed as more legitimate than bisexuals or pansexuals

- racism: one race is prioritized over another
- ableism: able bodies or able minds are seen as more prized and legitimate than disabled bodies and disabled minds
- sizeism: one standard body size or type is seen as healthy, acceptable, and worthy of sex and relationships
- ageism: an expectation of behavior based on age that comes with limitations and prejudice for any deviations
- cissexism: those who are cisgendered are seen as more legitimate than those who are transgendered
- singlism: single people are seen as lacking or less healthy than those who are in monogamous relationships
- normalism: normality is always sought above all else (Serano, 2013)

Constructed "-isms" build a wall of exclusion that obscures a real diverse self, because the assumed stereotypical traits of the category overshadow and limit the true traits of the individual, allowing no room for movement between identities. Certain labels and behavioral expressions skew how others interpret us. These very labels and identities "cancel out other qualities, reducing the complex person to a single attribute... It is precisely the variation among individuals that cultural categories trivialize and that representation often distorts" (Garland-Thomson, 1997, p. 12). A healthy, diverse, and always changing person becomes coded as a specific and limited type of person. All forms of identity and all categories of people experience sexuality and bodies differently, highlighting the extreme variations and diversity among all individuals. These binary labels mean loss of potential and motivation for people to transcend the limits of their category. This limits expectations from others and from oneself. And it's all based on universal assumptions of categories that obscure individuality or completely mislabel people.

To have a consistent, solid, and enduring identity (related to sexuality, gender, or sex) would require an immense amount of disattention and avoidance of acknowledging diversities. We cognitively search for data that allows us to place ourselves and others into sexually orientative gender and sex binaries with cognitive selection methods such as confirmation bias, which is the human tendency to look for and interpret information in a way that confirms one's expectations and preconceptions. How could homosexuality, heterosexuality, femaleness, or maleness take a single identifiable form in the brain when it takes such varied forms in people's lives? (Jordan-Young, 2010, p. x). We allow most data to fall outside the foreground of our perceptive processing, ignoring the vast terrain of similarities. When we use labels and categories, we lose all the overwhelming similarities.

Labels police individuals and are intended to exert power and control over their behavior and lifestyle. Determining someone to be hetero, female, kinky, or cisgendered is to reduce them to a container, allowing no room for evolution and defining their behaviors as caused by that identity. Anything done by someone who has been categorized as "gay" is assumed to be "gay" behavior that they are only doing because they are gay. Any label creates a border, which causes oppression via privilege and hierarchy. The boundaries of sexual-gender categories (stereotypes) require criteria for belonging, which inherently allows for discrimination and ambivalence.

Neutral activities are now co-opted and branded by labels. The elaborating (concretizing) of erotic preference (sexual interest) into a character (identity) attempts to set up norms, which creates a new binary. This is my issue with concepts like "female sexuality," "gay therapy," and other falsely identity-bound ideas. These inherently assume a universality of the identity, reducing the vast diversity within and whitewashing away all internal differences. The extension of one's identity to their entire life is reductionist and oppressive. This self-erasure is a "brutal reduction of the person to his sexual behaviors" (Bersani, 2010, p. 39).

There is little commonality between the experiences of a white, lower-income, neuroatypical, disabled, forty-something, lesbian, transsexual woman and a multiracial, high-income, thirty-something, able-bodied, neurotypical, heterosexual, cisgendered woman. They may have intersecting points of shared identity or experience, but no common culture, heritage, or social field. The erasure of all the other important and meaningful traits outside of their womanhood reduces them to one common theme. This is both oppressive and naïve. Apply this same issue to "gay," "man," or any other identity. There is a severe reduction of many components of the self outside the limits of identity.

These ideas are the same ones that have incapacitated women's sexualities. They have kept woman sexually passive and anxious about owning and bringing their own sexuality to an encounter. Instead, most female-bodied individuals have been socialized to wait to be approached for sex and then to allow themselves to be receptive to and empowered sexually by their partner. This is not being sexually active or confident. This gender binary–enforced style of sexuality creates far too many sexual-relational problems and low sexual self-esteem.

In the early twentieth century, sex became the determinant and qualifier for the basis of one's social identity, showing how identity is historically emergent, as all identities are situated within current political-historical dynamics. "Prior to that time, men and women...were categorically not heterosexuals. They didn't identify themselves as 'being' something called 'heterosexual.' They didn't think of themselves as having a 'straight' sexual identity, or indeed have any awareness that something called a 'sexual identity' even existed... Neither the terms nor the ideas that they express existed yet" (Blank, 2012, p. xiv).

"The word 'heterosexual,' like the word 'homosexual,' is simply a scientific adjective, historically and socially immature (less than 150 years old, in fact), and part of modernity's quest for order and rationality over the chaotic and irrational body" (Katz,

1996, p. 52). Homosexuality and heterosexuality are behaviors, not identities, and are neither stable nor coherent. There is nothing "essential" about labels. Heterosexuality, like all sexual identities, is a political and social affiliation and not a type of person. Those who do not fit into or feel at ease within a hetero or homo social ghetto feel such because their standards or interest are not aligned, thereby making group membership null and oppressive.

BOUND AND UNBOUND

Sex and gender place us within culture, determining where we will fit and how we will function. "Nearly every aspect of social life is organized by one's sex assignment—from schooling and relationships, to employment and religion, sports and entertainment, medicine and law" (Preves, 2008, p. 5). Gender is the first identity given to us at birth—and yes, it is *given* to us. We aren't born with a natural way of being sexual-relational or a core gender identity, but with desires and interests, and we are taught that these drives are sexual and accompanied by the social qualifier of an identity and its related expectations. Identities are repeated performances that congeal over time to produce the appearance of substance, of a natural sort of being (Butler, 1990). Sex and relationships are where gender rules are most salient and overt. The role of "man" leads to the consequences of dying sooner, being more at risk for disease, having higher suicide rates, more alcoholism, a higher propensity toward crime, and more dangerous jobs. This is due to the pressures that come with the expectations of this gender label.

When we refer to "sexuality" or "gender," we are talking about a bound identity, imprisoning gender and sexual behaviors. The very concept of determining sex requires that we ignore sameness to focus only upon differences. "Each of us unavoidably re-creates stereotypes every time we use the words 'man' or 'woman'...therefore, each time we speak or write 'woman,' we evoke the dual-gender system as a psycho-social-political structure that divides human possibility between two categories" (Dimen, 2003, p. 73). This applies to use of the words "gay" and "straight" as well. The tyranny of language and labels both form and sustain who we are to ourselves and others. "Female" and "male" preferences are marketed to you and are products of social-cultural constructions of gender. An unbound identity is one that "contests the attribution of any character to masculinity and femininity" (Hird, 2008a, p. 233). We also search for the cues that determine one's "sex" as assigned arbitrarily by culture. We cannot actually see sex anatomy, or genitals, so we look instead for "cultural genitals."

We have the concepts of gender and sex as enduring permanently regardless of alteration, which is clinically called "gender permanence." Surgeries, such as anatomy and genital change, never allow the individual to be fully a new self, but instead one that is juxtaposed with their former self, so their identity is maintained in this tension of old versus new. Both gender change and orthodontics are permanent, yet only the transgendered person is still held accountable to his or her original birth body. Changing one's face or body (nose job, face lift, tummy tuck, breast implants, tooth veneers, vaginal rejuvenation, etc.), hair color, skin tone, and weight are all allowable and integrated, but changing one's genitals requires doctors' approval, therapeutic obstacles, and social stigma. There is no "age identity disorder" (for those who feel younger than they look and want to use anti-aging medications, products, and surgeries), but gender is once again a special case rife with anxiety and always held in the healthy-versus-unhealthy binary. Changing race, age, or body composition is supported and not made deviant, but challenging one's sex or gender upsets society and becomes over-regulated. Plastic surgery offices do not demand therapy or therapist permission in exchange for a new face or body, but the offices that work medically and therapeutically are basically sex control centers. "Sex assignment surgeries 'don't count' as a legitimate biological transformation, given that sex difference is singled out among all the various parts of the body as the irreducible essence of a person" (A. Friedman, 2013, p. 50).

GENDER KILLS

Gender is not in crisis but carries with it inherent damage to both men and women. The male gender is arbitrarily discriminated against with actions such as being drafted to war (the male-only draft demonstrates that the male body is seen as disposable, with less right to life), being circumcised (although it is illegal in the United States for females), having their sexuality brutalized with psychology (faux diagnoses such as "intimacy disorders" and "sex addiction"), and, for no reason at all, "men" are last to get saved from a sinking ship ("women and children first," because again, having a penis makes one more disposable).

These dehumanizing examples based on one's genitals extend to females as well. Women, due to nothing but their genitals, are expected to give up their career and interests to be the primary child caregiver and have much higher incidence of body policing (culture reinforces body norms and expectations of a constructed and limited "femininity" such as hairlessness, youthfulness, and thinness), not to mention how the media perpetuates the idea that a woman's only life goals ought to be marriage and children. There is no valid basis for these expectations and ideologies; they are socially constructed and maintained.

"The pattern of seeking a biological or natural basis to justify inequalities of sex (just as with race and class, as racism operates from the same process) is repeated…in discursive and institutionalized practices such as eugenics, social Darwinism, Nazism,

[and] IQ testing" (Sturgeon, 2009, p. 21). These "natural" justifications for social inequalities continue. Our views on nature and gender tell us far more about our culture than about our biology or what is "natural."

Etiquette is disempowerment due to genitals, and it perpetuates sexism, separation, and belittlement. "Men do not exit the womb knowing they will one day have to buy a date a corsage or spend two months' income to buy an engagement ring. Rules on everything, from who pays for the date or rehearsal dinner to who leads while dancing, drives the car, cooks dinner, or initiates sex, all serve to regulate heterosexual practice" (Ingraham, 2008, p. 7). These standards are both arbitrary and damaging, as many feel they have no other options. All standards are negotiable, and any "rules" based on gender should be challenged. All of this sexism is due to the existence and maintenance of gender, and it does nothing but create damage.

Masculinity harms both genders, as neither is allowed to create the identity and lifestyle they may want. We must "stop dividing the sexes into the disposable sex vs. the protected sex" (Farrell, 1993, p. 229). All sexes and genders have the same value and worth, and as such neither should be made to give up their seat or always pay the dinner bill. Buffet-style gender divisions, which means accepting and allowing gender-role expectations and etiquette only when they work in your favor, perpetuate the negative expectations and gender violence as well.

The creation of an other—an "opposite" sex—builds distance and anxiety when engaging and in relationships with this mysterious "opposite." This is what leads to gender violence, such as rape. The culturally enforced male disposition of aggression and dominance, combined with the enforced female disposition of being peaceful and nurturing, set us all up for dangerous tensions. Getting rid of gender allows for all individuals to pick and choose from all traits, and also leads to an increased comfort with the other, as similarities are acknowledged.

THE SCIENCE OF SEX

Psychology has pathologized the "experiences of 'fluid boundaries,' 'unstable egos,' [and] 'multiplicity' of selfhood" (Watkins & Shulman, 2008, p. 163). The mental health field expects consistency and stability. Outwardly there are many recognizable cultural signs of gender, but internally we are not gendered in terms of organs, cells, or fat. "We never graduate from working on identity; we simply rework with the materials at hand" (Turkle, 2011, p. 158).

We have Western clitoral and penis size standards for infants. The medical field utilizes a phallus scale to determine what is too big to be allowed to be a clitoris and what is too small to be allowed to be a penis. If a penis is too small (a micropenis) or a clitoris is too large (a clitoral hypertrophy), the medical protocol is for the individual to be "corrected" (mutilated) to be made "normal." The clitoris is trimmed back, even though it is fully functional, and the penis, not considered socially acceptable in size, would lead to the child being assigned as female (ignoring chromosomal and gonadal composition) (Preves, 2008, p. 56). The sex and gender we decide to force upon a child are determined by our ideas of what is "normal" and "correct." From a primitive heteromatrix of only intercourse as sex, penis size may matter, but this is a limited view, as is butchering a "too large" clitoris in the interest of creating "normality."

"Labeling someone a man or a woman is a social decision… The more we look for a simple physical basis for 'sex,' the more it becomes clear that 'sex' is not a pure physical category" (Fausto-Sterling, 2000, p. 3). There are many naturally occurring biosexual diversities such as Turner syndrome, Klinefelter syndrome, androgen insensitivity syndrome, congenital adrenal hyperplasia, intersex, females who are genetically males, and males who are genetically females (L. Davis, 2013b). In fact, there are between five and twenty biological sexes—certainly not only two. Anne Fausto-Sterling describes the five sexes as male, female, herms (true), merms (male pseudo), and ferms (female pseudo).

"If a child is born with two X chromosomes, oviducts, ovaries, and a uterus on the inside, but a penis and scrotum on the outside…is this child a boy or a girl?" (Fausto-Sterling, 2000, p. 5). All of these potentialities are considered "disorders" by the medical community because they do not fit neatly into the gender binary of being either male or female. The labeling of these differences as pathology and their subsequent treatments are both psychologically and sexually abusive.

The perpetuated idea that there are two discrete genders and sexes denies the reality that there are a multitude of both. The true reality is the diverse existence of: chromosomal XY, XX, XO, X (Turner syndrome), XXY (Klinefelter syndrome), XXXY, XXYY, XXXYY, and there are those that have the internal anatomy (gonads) of ovaries, testes, or a combo, with unexpected external genitalia, where the external body has a penis, but the internal has ovaries or vice versa. Biosexual reality challenges the tyranny of XX and XY as male or female only.

MEN ARE NOT FROM MARS

This concept, and all the related books, perpetuate misogyny (the dislike of women) and misandry (the dislike of men), ignorantly perpetuating gender violence and confusion. The mythic assumed categories of "man" and "woman" are not as distinct and separate as believed. There are no "opposite" sexes. "Humans are actually one of a number of 'weakly dimorphic' species" (A. Friedman, 2013, p. 4). There are similarities, differences, and complements, but not "opposites." "One of the most damaging and nefarious lies is that men and woman are different when it comes to sex and dating" (Mukhopadhyay, 2011, p. 20).

Masculinity and femininity are merely constructed from a set of beliefs. We all live with psychosocial belief systems that enable us to articulate what constitutes a man and a woman on a stereotypical level, and to judge whether others' and our own masculinity and femininity are appropriate (Stoller, 1985). These sexual and gendered bodies carry expectations and about conduct, fashion, temperament, and social roles.

But much sameness actually exists, and the "diversity" model—as opposed to a "difference" model—demonstrates this flawed concept because there is as much internal difference between "men" as there is between a "man" and a "woman." "The state and legal system has an interest in maintaining only two sexes, but our collective biological bodies do not... There are many other bodies...that evidently mix together anatomical components conventionally attributed to both males and females... Nature really offers us more than two sexes" (Fausto-Sterling, 2000, p. 31).

These intrasex differences and intersex similarities make extinct the notion of sex differences such as a "male sexuality" and a "female sexuality." "Males and females are much more genetically similar than different" (A. Friedman, 2013, p. 216). Genetic difference is less than 1 percent, as males and females are genetically 99 percent identical (S. Richardson, 2010, p. 6). "Yet the cultural notion of 'opposite' sexes expands that 1 percent difference to 100 percent... Only by social measures are we more different than similar" (A. Friedman, 2013, p. 4).

There is as much difference between men and men, gay and gay, as there are between men and women, gay and heterosexual. Identity politics reinforces separation and a sense of difference. Any identification of "female" or "male" is a compromise, as everyone has attributes outside these designations.

NATURE IS QUEER

Many look to nature to find sexual-relational truth, yet nature provides no answer because it is very queer and diverse. Psychology and sexology too often look to socially constructed versions of "nature" to determine what is "natural" and therefore "healthy." Their scientific version of natural and healthy is based on myth and fantasy, as nature is a metaphor. The researchers looking at nature often bring with them a normative expectation, and with this they rule out any non-hetero sexuality as illegitimate. Anything non-procreative and non-hetero is seen as a pathological outcome, either environmentally or biologically.

Darwin's sexual selection theories are used obsessively to legitimize sexist and anti-alternative theories of relationship and sex, yet they are all based on a heterosexual reproductive model of sexual-relational behavior. These theories ignore that not everyone is hetero (there are millions of sexual orientations, some not directed toward other people at all, and instead toward the self or other objects), sexual (asexuality exists), desiring of reproduction (not all sex is for procreation, and not all people want children), and wanting dyadic partnership (some are polyamorous or non-monogamous), and that there are far more than just two genders. Darwin and evolutionary psychology's antiquated work "converge to make reproduction the privileged, unique, and sole aim of sex... It excludes or suppresses from the evidence much of what animals actually do: autosexual behaviors, nonreproductve sexual intercourse between males and females, same-sex behaviors... It is by means of these exclusions and suppressions that heterosexuality...comes to be equated with "nature" (Lancaster, 2003, p. 85).

Animals and plants are nature and therefore all that they do and all that occurs with them is natural. Animals of the same sex are sexual, court each other, pair bond, and co-parent. The plant and animal kingdoms contain a wealth of natural diversity. The reality is that human life is closer to nature in that both contain intersexuality, transsexualism, and transvestism. "Most species on this planet are not sexually dimorphic… [indicating a] prolific abundance of sex diversity" (Hird, 2004, p. 12). This means that much of nature does not live up to the mythic human expectation of two sexes and genders only. Humans and animals both "live in a polysexual, polygendered world" (Bagemihl, 1999, p. 7). Plants, most fungi, and fish can be intersex (Bagemihl, 1999; Hird, 2004; Roughgarden, 2013), many plants and aquatic animals are transsexual, and many insects become transvestites. Asexuality is also seen among animals, as virtually every animal population includes non-breeding individuals. "Low sexual desire," where male animals stay separate from females, and with "refusal" and "indifference" they "make no sexual contact or reproduce" (Bagemihl, 1999, p. 16) demonstrates the diversity of sexual arousals in the animal kingdom.

There are many myths about gender that the animal, plant, and aquatic (as well as human) worlds dispel. These other species teach us that in nature:

1. An organism is *not* solely male or female for life, and there are more than just two genders/sexes. Some animals start out as one gender and then change into the opposite. Nature shows us "animals with females that become males, animals with no males at all, animals that are both male and female simultaneously, animals where females resemble males. Many animals live without two distinct genders or with multiple genders" (Bagemihl, 1999, p. 36). There are even some fish that "are both genders at the same time… These simultaneous hermaphrodites change between male and female roles several times as they mate" (Roughgarden, 2013, p. 33). Again and again, nature demonstrates the fluidity and inconsistency of gender.

2. Animals can be asexual. This is demonstrated most clearly with parthenogenesis, where a species has the ability to make a genetic copy of itself and reproduce without sex or sperm (Hird, 2004, and Bagemihl, 1999).
3. Animals display transvestism. "Sex role reversal definitely occurs in nature" (Roughgarden, 2013, p. 47). Animals have been shown to mimic the mating behaviors of the opposite gender.
4. Males can have XX chromosomes and females can have XY.
5. Animals have sex purely for pleasure. Sex that does not or cannot lead to reproduction occurs. Masturbation, non-penetrative sex, oral sex, and anal sex are all found in the animal kingdom (Hird, 2004; Bagemihl, 1999).
6. Some male animals prefer monogamy while the females want to be polyamorous. "Lifelong monogamy is rare, even within monogamous species" (Roughgarden, 2013, p. 28).
7. Same-sex couples, bisexuality, and same-sex parenting exist. "Animals of the same gender often interact with each other...organized around five major behavioral categories: courtship, affection, sex, pair-bonding, and parenting" (Bagemihl, 1999, p. 12). In addition, as with humans, bisexual and heterosexual species show an erotic fluidity where their sexual orientation toward same and opposite genders changes, with periods of homosexuality and heterosexuality.

AROUSAL IS A CONSTELLATION

Sex exists within an assumed system of easily differentiated parts. The system of sexual orientation includes the erroneous idea that "the most salient way we can classify a person's psychoerotic system is with respect to the gender of the object he or she eroticizes" (Schwartz, 1995, p. 115). LGBT identities are based on an obsession with the gender of an individual's sexual object choice. But sexuality extends far beyond gender and object choice, and is often expressed without the use of genitals. With identity and sexuality not being fixed or essential, our sexual-relational identity is chosen daily and even momentarily, always within a social, relational, and historical context. Our culture forces us to oppressively identify and choose in a continual process of self-reconstruction via engagement and dialogue whether we realize it or not.

Many theoretical perspectives "endorse sexual stability and implicitly devalue erotic flexibility and mobility…[and] tend to call indeterminacy a type of 'confusion'… None of these writers makes room…for an individual who might be better off without imagining that he or she needs a sexual 'orientation' at all… The claim that erotic stability exists and, even more improbably, that it is a hallmark of health and virtue is seriously problematic" (Schwartz, 1995, p. 121). "We continually seek to discover the truth of the individual… We find ourselves engaging in identity work in order to stabilize who we are… We are forced to identify with something…some category of identity that is determined outside of us… One's self is not ever established for good, but must be continually expressed and reconstituted" (Pitts-Taylor, 2007, p. 161). Identity is an escape from freedom.

Sexualities are not a "matter of either-or. Nor are they fixed… They are emergent contingencies. Most individuals experience their sexuality as revealed…maybe an ongoing process… There is more to anyone's sexual preference than meets the eye at any given moment" (Dimen, 2003, p. 117). Arousal and orientation targets have many possible axes that intersect, and all can be very plastic, meaning sexual interests and what arouses you can change and evolve. And sexual interests and orientations are about far more than just gender choice. It is impossible to create a taxonomy that is inclusive of all sexual arousal interests. Anything and everything can be sexualized.

The major categories of arousal are based upon:

1. Human———Object———None (asexual)

Sexual orientation and interest can be directed at other humans, toward non-human objects, and even at times toward nothing and no one at all. The vast variety of what can be found to be arousing is what makes sexuality so creative and fascinating. There is no "right" direction for arousal, as healthy sex is about being confident in what turns you on and finding healthy ways to engage with your full sexual constellation.

2. Self (auto-mono-sexual)———Other——— None (asexual)

Targets of sexual arousal take further direction toward either the self or another, and sometimes toward neither. Some individuals are most aroused by watching themselves, either having sex or masturbating. Sex is not always about having an other.

3. Opposite "Gender"———Ambiguous——— Same "Gender"

Individuals can be aroused by their same gender, the opposite gender, those of ambiguous gender, or both genders. And these interests can change over time depending on who you meet and due to the incorporation and intersection of other arousal interests. Looking for a fixed or enduring sexuality often ignores sexual fluidity and the possibilities for learning about new and creative sexual interests. In service of this, choose to leave your sexuality and sexual identity as "in progress," "under development," and "to be continued."

4. Specificity: age, height, body shape, hair color

Body-based factors can play a role in sexual-relational partner choice. The power of ornamental anatomy in eroticism can be prioritized to become the main focal point of sex.

5. Psycho-moral and situation: shame, guilt, disgust, anxiety, domination, submission

Psychology and feelings are easily eroticized and can be used as part of many individuals' arousal constellations. The creation of certain scenarios and situations can fold another layer of arousal into sexuality. Acknowledging the power of environment to create specific emotional tensions and dynamics allows for altered sexual states and heightened arousal. As long as sex is consensual and no one is injured, then it's all part of healthy sexual expression.

6. Danger/Taboo: force, bareback, body modification, impact play, age regression

Engaging with sexuality that creates risk and operates on the edges of safety is very common. These edges amp up tension and anxiety, both of which are read neurologically as arousing. My advice with these forms of sex play is to get educated and also to find a mentor to show you how to be sexually safe. As with all forms of sex, even the basics, sexual skills are learned, *not* innate or inborn, and require practice and experience. Sex is no more obvious or natural than skill with sports, academics, or science. All involve study, practice, and passion.

These themes and categories are far from an exhaustive list of all that can arouse. Explore which themes and behaviors you may not have considered sexually and find ways to fold them into your sexuality for heightened arousal. If any of them make you nervous, try weaving them in slowly by discussing them, fantasizing about them, masturbating to the fantasy, or viewing erotica that plays them out. Having a full spectrum of sexual interest will help lay a strong erotic foundation for both long-term sustainable partnered sex and a vibrant individual sex life.

It's important to not shame certain sexual forms and interests as "primitive" or "childish"; sex is not able to be separated into constructed categories such as "mature" and "immature." Arousal has no interest in these made-up distinctions. Much sexuality is inherent from birth and childhood, and then continues into adulthood. "We have less conscious control over our fantasies and sexual predilections than we would wish to believe" (Kahr, 2008, p. 396). The permitting of our full sexualities and the willingness to grow by exploring new sexual terrain is the only sign of maturity. Healthy individuals do not hide sexual parts of themselves due to a partner's discomfort. Working through sexual anxiety is part of being in a relationship. Healthy sex is sex that is never led or diminished by someone else's anxiety.

PRIDE IS PROBLEMATIC; LIBERATION BY AMPUTATION

LGBT politics attempt to concretize and maintain polarizing and minimizing labels. This works to "flatten difference to achieve equality" (Garland-Thomson, 1997, p. 17) by amputating those members who will not assimilate or who maintain aspects of themselves that the group finds marginalizing or inappropriate. Battles for equality cannot be won using the same tools the oppressive culture itself has used. "The new homonormativity—it is a politics that does not contest dominant heteronormative assumptions and institutions, but upholds and sustains them while promising…depoliticized gay culture anchored in domesticity" (Duggan, 2002, p. 176). Conventional notions of gay rights rely on a construction of assimilation that leaves existing structures intact, ignoring the fact that "the master's tools will never dismantle the master's house" (Lorde, 2007, p. 110). This assimilationist anti-difference ideology, while purporting to have an

> emphasis on appreciating difference because "we are all the same" can negate the celebration of difference… While espousing a politic of valuing diversity, the message frequently asserted is, conversely, that those outside the heterosexual mainstream are "ok" because they are *normal* and *just like everyone else*. If difference is only celebrated because it matches the status quo, then it is assimilation rather than difference that is actually being celebrated. (Stafford, 2009, p. 177)

"The framework in which queer families' alternative non-normative family styles are expected to exist is one that shows how normal they are despite their obvious difference" (Evans, 2009, p. 235). "Gays" and other individuals who identify as non-normative sexually and relationally have finally earned the right to their marginal and sometimes non-dyadic alternative relational styles and sexual-relational identities. But some prejudice is now becoming turned around to inflict the same historical prejudice upon non-normative members of their own community and identity. This attempt at whitewashing difference is a defensive "othering" (when the marginalized person attempts to emulate the hegemonic norm [Campbell, 2009, p. 24]) and a form of internalized homophobia. "The desire to emulate the Other (the norm) establishes and maintains a wide gap between those who are loathed and that which is desired" (p. 25).

In reference to institutions like marriage, "the structures of heteronormativity, and the various violences these structures and discourses entail, do not necessarily disappear when the sexuality of the participants is changed... We also have to think about the institution itself... It is an economic institution. It is about property. It is not about human relations" (A. Davis, 2012, p. 161). As such, a diversity of family and relationships is healthy and needed. But the fear of acknowledging difference is far from eliminated. We need to move away from the "we are all the same" mentality, because we are not. Children raised in diverse families are not the same, they are diverse. Studies on children of gay and non-normative parents and families show that they do turn out different—and healthier. The outcomes of the studies "highlight in children growing up with lesbian/gay parents less traditional gender-typing; higher self-esteem and better mental health; more egalitarian, shared parenting; more closeness and communication between parents and children; and increased awareness and empathy in children towards social diversity" (R. Epstein, 2009, p. 15).

The LGBT community has its own hierarchy, and chooses who is fought for and who is left outside. Many political issues only serve the wealthier, white, male populations, leaving outside the queer, lower economic status, and the racially diverse. The marriage fight "fails to address the fundamental problem of marriage as an official enforcement of the hierarchy of sexual deviance, creating a two-class system in which the conventional sexuality of the monogamous couple (whether straight or gay) is upheld as the fundamental unit of society, at the expense of unconventional family units and those who are not monogamous or whose sexuality is unconventional in other ways" (Wilkerson, 2011, p. 206). Liberation movements become enforcers of the same sort of oppressive status quo they have tried to escape. "I believe it is profoundly unethical…to purchase 'my' liberation at the cost of another's oppression… It is the way in which previously marginalized groups become the enforcers of other people's marginalization" (Jennings, 2013, p. 7).

"This strategy of bringing into the fold those who can fit in the box called 'respectability'…still [excludes] those who do not" (Jennings, 2013, p. 7). Identity regulates the sexual body and sexual psyche, thereby being unethical and anti-self. The psychosocial and sexual-relational self-defense of a post-identity queer subjectivity's "seemingly liberatory categories…may [itself] become tied to (oppressive) regulatory regimes and practices" (Hodges, 2008, p. 8). Gender-specific behaviors are born from expectations and rules, not our hormones or anatomy, as demonstrated with different expressions via history and culture. Identity leads to stereotypes and false understandings. True intimacy is not about knowledge of identification. We can relate and connect deeply with others without identifying them. "Identity categories tend to be instruments of regulatory regimes" (Butler, 1991, p. 13).

LIBERATED SEX

Liberated sexuality would be a complex field of "the nomad…a non-unitary…multi-layered vision…the perverse hybridization" (Braidotti, 2011, p. 5). This would ignore the search for concrete, enduring truths of the "essentialists…[who claim] in a rather simple-minded way that being a woman or an ethnic minority [is] somehow rooted in the body. That identity [is] tied to the body, written on the body" (L. Davis, 2013a, p. 265). Similar to this is the typical transgenderism that is reliant upon the idea of an essential maleness or femaleness, and the materiality of a truly male or female body. As a construction, we can transform, ignore, and liberate ourselves from it.

IDENTITY EQUALS OPPRESSION

Both heterosexuality and homosexuality are social and political identities, far more than orientations. Individuals must *learn* and be *taught* heterosexuality and homosexuality. "We frequently refer to heterosexuality as something that is naturally occurring, overlooking the myriad ways we have *learned* how to practice heterosexuality…the ways in which ascribed behaviors for women and men…actually organize the institution of heterosexuality" (Ingraham, 2005, p. 1). Sexual identity, like any identity, is performative. Homosexuality is a cultural practice and is not limited to men, or men who have sex with men, but is open for anyone to participate in and identify with (Halperin, 2012). Remember that sexual orientation is far larger than homo versus hetero, and that identity and orientation are two very different categories of being. That's why there is no "heterosexual" or "homosexual"; it's a socially constructed way of being, thinking, and relating. No one is born understanding their sexual culture; it must be taught. "It is not enough for a man to be homosexual in order to be gay. Same-sex desire alone does not equal gayness. In order to be gay, a man has to learn to relate to the world around him in a distinctive way… 'Gay' refers not just to something you *are*, but also something you *do*. Which means that you don't have to be homosexual to do it. Gay culture does not appeal exclusively to those with a same-sex erotic preference" (Halperin, 2012, p. 13).

Erotic plasticity, which is a neurological, psychological, and social process, explains how sexuality, including an understanding of identity and interest in sexual behaviors, is a "queering" of sex, an ever-changing and ever-evolving fluid sexuality. Identities and sexualities should be created in an open process of self-invention that does not involve an inherited understanding. Identities are not linear, but nonlinear dynamic fluid systems. "Identities are complex. We don't just have just one…we can alter—add or subtract—identities. We make choices about which identity or identities are made into a core part of our self-definition and which will be treated as 'threads' or secondary" (Seidman, 2002, p. 9).

Sexuality is an emergence, whereas diagnoses and identities imply endpoints and permanent final resting points versus episodes in an unstable chain of events (Hook, 2007, p. 157). "Identity crises" are the expected signs of health and evolution, and "stable" identities pose far larger psychological issues. The bravery arises when one is resolute in actively protesting against the confinement of labels. This liberation is "an invitation to disidentify ourselves from the sedentary phallogocentric monologism…to start cultivating the art of disloyalty to civilization… that form of healthy disrespect for both academic and intellectual conventions" (Braidotti, 2011, p. 24).

What are we then? We have subjectivity, born from our current time, place, relationship, and our master narrative of self. This is in constant flux. We therefore have many subjectivities, multiple personalities. Our current categories and identifiers are far too limited and rigid to encompass and explain individuals' total selves accurately without minimizing, misdirecting, shaming, or abandoning them. The need to separate subjectivity from identity is due to identity leading to both overidentification and disidentification.

GENDER AS TRAUMA

Gender identity confusion is a healthy part of development. We should all feel unsure, confused, and dysphoric about committing to a gender, given all the rules and expectations that are carried along with it. Being solid about gender identity is the true disorder. There is much health in gender identity refusal and disinterest. This intersects with the concepts of personality styles as well. "Personality is a problem…because it indicates rigidity… Personality is…a social problem with social origins and effects… Socially produced aspects of identity…impede self-reflection, agency, autonomy… Personality is something to be transcended" (Fox et al., 2009, p. 68), with the goal of moving beyond it. "Internal life [is] a historical production, a creation emerging in the field of power relations as these are presented in language… Human subjectivity is…contingent, constituted culturally and politically through language" (Dimen, 2003, p. 78). Language is where selves and their identities are created. We must be more sensitive to the labels and languaging we use to describe and encapsulate ourselves.

"All object choice and gender identities are to be understood…as problematic, trauma-based, defensive psychic constructions" (Domenici & Lesser, 1995, p. 34). There is a defense and power struggle in all identities and object choices. We choose partners from our lowest and most primitive selves—I'll let you enact your issues and you let me enact mine, and we will call it a match. Our need to immerse ourselves into a group, internalize groupthink and standards, lose our individuality is what Erich Fromm calls an "escape *from* freedom." Immersion into groups and the related groupthink always leads to dangerous conformity, and gender is no different. Early childhood sexual segregation plays an important role in the creation and maintenance of gender and gender norms. "Childhood play steers boys and girls onto disparate paths… Gender differences emerge in early childhood and exert their influence throughout life… Early on, each sex will stereotype the other in ways that make them seem…strange and alien to the other" (Barnett & Rivers, 2004, p. 219). The gender rules of our culture get reenacted and strengthened through social play. Our associative minds pick up and internalize repeated experiences of being taught and shown how our sex should perform. Television, magazines, and family members all model for us how our gender is expected to act. There is nothing natural or essential with gender or gender performance.

The work is about evolving out of an identity and stopping the problematic over-identification with one's "category." The undoing of fixed essential gender and sexual identity allow for this process to take place. Subjectivity is the fluid, relational, and contextual space in which one can reconstruct oneself constantly.

Individuals have many selves, and "our identities are multi-layered and constructed in interaction with other human agents, even though we are often expected…to present our identity as a 'unitary self'… These 'coherent selves' can never be anything but fictional" (F. Jung, 2008, p. 20).

Gender can be conceptualized as:

1. Desire to be the "other": which plays off of and maintains the gender binary (seeing self as man/woman and wanting to be "opposite")
2. Hybrid: where one sees oneself as a combination or mixture of both or all genders
3. Non-conforming: where one is none and neither and does not adhere to any notion of gender
4. Queer: where one does not relate to any current prescribed identity and creates a fluid and subjective original identity of self

"Fundamentally, we are relational beings. We don't live in isolation; our entire lives are lived in a matrix of relationships. We are born into relationships and we live out our lives in relationships… Our personalities take on their unique forms and colorations through the multitude of experiences that, as human beings, we have in relationships" (Kingma, 1998, p. 11).

"Beneath the layer of socialization...is not a true self, but 'a multiple, shifting, and often self-contradictory identity made up of heterogeneous and heteronomous representations' [Rivera, 1989, p. 27]. And beneath the layer of gender enculturation is not an essential gender, but an ambiguous, variably constructed, highly conflicted relation to one's sex" (Dimen, 2003, p. 80). "The motivation to explore nomadic subjectivity comes from the conviction that, in these times of accelerating changes, many traditional points of reference and age-old habits of thought are being recomposed... At such a time more conceptual creativity is necessary" (Braidotti, 2011, p. 13). Bordo finalizes the concept: "as people alter, expand, and experiment with—surgically and otherwise—the bodily forms that constitute our repertoire of sexual possibilities...the categories inevitably will become inadequate" (1999, p. 41).

Talk about people or gender conceptually, as multiplicitous, incongruent, and diverse, not about "gays" or "women" as distinct people. "The point is not just mere deconstruction, but the relocation of identities on new grounds that account for multiple belongings" (Braidotti, 2011, p. 10). Don't diagnose or label anyone, especially a child, with gender so as to allow gender self-determination, and don't refer to others as boys and girls, so as to resist gender stereotyping and allow for cross-gender exploration (Ward, 2012b). Let's be more like other, more advanced cultures, such as Sweden, where a gender-neutral pronoun has been legitimized by being added to the Swedish dictionary: *hand* = he; *hon* = she; *hen* = gender neutral. "In English there are no good words, no easy words. All the language we have created—transgender, transsexual...FTM, MTF—places us in relationship to masculine and feminine, between the two, combining the two, moving from one to the other" (Clare, 2003, p. 260).

Gender health comes with allowing for choice and fluid change via gender self-determination versus the damaging imposition and expectations of gender diagnosing. No one needs to choose a label at all. "Gender identity disorder" is actually ordered and healthy. I'm more inclined to give the diagnosis of a "disorder" around gender to those that readily accept one or the other. "Categories of difference are ultimately that which must be transcended—erased—if we are to ascend into the treasured neutrality of humanity" (Winnubst, 2006, p. 18).

Case Study: Sam

In my sex therapy practice I am fortunate enough to get to work with individuals who are exploring their gender and sexuality. Often these clients come in unsure about who they are and who they want to be. Sam came in years ago and said, "I'm not sure if I'm meant to be the gender I was born, and so I don't know how to identify myself." The very idea that Sam had to *choose* a gender and then stick with it was the actual issue, not *which* gender to choose.

We explored the reality that gender was a socially created category, and that any gender, outside of just male or female, was available for use, or none at all. I explained to Sam that to be a gender carries with it certain expectations, and that these create problems for many people.

CHAPTER 10.

THE FUTURE OF SEX AND RELATIONSHIPS

SEXUAL DARK AGES

The future equals the death of relationships (marriage), death of the family (as paternal and determined by birth), and death of sex (identities, labels, boundaries, hierarchy). It's the death of a future as comfortably defined by tradition and ritual. It's "the dissolution of everything we understand as 'solid and recognizable'" (Edelman, 2004, p. 37). "Popular culture has already imagined multiple alternatives to male and female, masculine and feminine, family and individuality, and…can provide a rich archive for an alternative politics of embodiment, reproduction and non-reproduction" (Halberstam, 2008, p. 266). Pleasure, intimacy, and community are freed from biological and social constructions and confines. New sexual-relational norms and configurations will create a crisis for traditional heteronormative ideals and ways of being.

Freedom historically "was focused upon combating old forms of authority and restraint… Although man has rid himself from old enemies of freedom, new enemies of a different nature have arisen; enemies which are not essentially external restraints, but internal factors blocking the full realization of the freedom of personality" (Fromm, 1969, p. 104). After doing the work of shedding the standards and norms of sexual policing from the outside, one must continue to examine the bondage created internally.

Many in our culture are trying to run twenty-first-century ideas and values on outdated sexual-relational templates and norms. They need to be updated to include the current available sexual-relational technologies such as computer and phone apps.

> Technology has changed, is changing, and will continue to change how humans experience sexual and romantic relationships… Humans have always sought to sexualize technology and to technologize sex… We bring technology into the bedroom… The Internet has done more to help us upgrade our sex lives than any other technology in history… Sex is one of the primary drivers of technological innovation, and we eventually assimilate every new communications technology into our relationships. (Lynn, 2005, p. 2)

More evolution is needed, as many live in the "sexual dark ages," refusing to take their sexuality online. Regardless of the many pitfalls, online is where relationshipping is headed, and it serves us to learn how to navigate online sex and work with the anxieties it produces. One of the many gifts of Internet sexuality is the decentering and globalization of relationships and sex.

The notion that cyber-relationships are less real or not "reality" at all is a misunderstanding of the true intimacy that online relationships possess. "Online relationships develop differently than offline relationships, progressing from the inside out" (Lynn, 2005, p. 58), and often allow for more psychological and emotional depth due to the reliance on verbal communication and sharing. "Such a novel psychological reality…is defined by the various psychological interactions occurring in it… Cyberspace is not virtual… Cyberspace is a part of reality: it is, therefore, incorrect to regard it as the direct opposite of real space. Cyberspace is part of real space, and online relationships are real relationships" (Ben-Ze'ev, 2004, p. 2). I do advise individuals who want a physical relationship to meet as soon as possible. Cyber-relationships can exist in fantasy projections only, where the other acts as a blank screen upon which we can project our desire of how we wish them to be, whereas meeting face-to-face, with eye contact and the inclusion of touch, forces more of a recognition of who the other is.

SEX IN THE NOW

"Coercive belief in the paramount value of the future" (Edelman, 2004, p. 4) and a fantasy-based structure guides most sex and relationships. But always planning and running with an eye toward the future leaves the now behind. Process is ignored in service of the telos of partnership or family. Arousing sex and fun relationships need to be "queered" and ignore a future-orientation paired with a modernist belief in individual and relational consistency. Not doing so fails to acknowledge that we are ever-changing systems and that no one will be able to predict longevity or long-term compatibility. Relational decision-making must be based on a present-oriented paradigm. A futuristic lens is a fantasy lens, and this fantasy of what sex or marriage will create or provide is truly unknown. Yet this future focus drives breakups, second dates, and marital proposals.

A new relational mode challenges us to get comfortable and create new methods of relationshipping. We are on a new course, and it requires new knowledge and comfort with new boundaries and styles of relationality. New sexual-social modes will require new sexual-relational role models for newer generations to learn from. This sexual-social learning requires both identification and imitation (A. Green, 2014, p. viii), as well as liberation from oppressive sexual-relational norms with new subjectivities and visions. "Rather than searching for stereotypical norms, liberation psychologies place stress on identifying, supporting, and nurturing the psychological attempts of individuals and groups alike to re-author their own sense of identity. This requires a critical analysis of oppressive power relations, including those in psychology itself" (Watkins & Shulman, 2008, p. 5).

"Thrive in the destabilization and disruption of normalizing discourses of family, gender, and compulsory heterosexuality. It's an upbringing that encourages stability in mobility, security in change, clarity in ambiguity… Multiculturalism and multi-sexualism are normative constructions" (Pallotta-Chiarolli, 1999, p. 72).

SEX TECH

Current technology has had a huge impact, both positive and negative, on relationships and sexuality, creating a "playful and pleasure-prone relationship to technology that is not based on functionality" (Braidotti, 2013, p. 91). A better understanding of the impact will mitigate the possible consequences. Social media is our newest form of romantic cocaine, allowing for ubiquitous snorting of our sexual other at any immediate time or place. "We look to technology for ways to be in relationships and protect ourselves from them at the same time" (Turkle, 2011, p. xii). Individuals must learn how to use sex technology to appropriately and effectively achieve our relational and sexual goals, and how to navigate relational boundaries in this new millennium when our social life online is oftentimes more active than our lives out in the world.

"Sexual cyborgs" speaks to the technology that is now folded into sexuality and relationality and has freed it. Technology has truly liberated sex. The future presents us with more options and fluidity. Sex is now also separated and decentered from committed relationships. Rigid assumptions and structures around relating will be deconstructed and reappropriated. A good example is liberated reproduction, where technology has removed sex from reproduction and reproduction from sex. To procreate is no longer a requirement, and sex can be had just for fun. Advances will continue to allow for reproduction without sex, thereby freeing women from the oppression of reproduction and motherhood.

The globalization of both sex and relating due to computer and phone apps have expanded partner choices. Geographic sexual boundaries no longer exist, as all areas and populations are now reachable quickly and efficiently on smart phones and other devices. Whereas at one time sex and dating were limited to whoever lived nearby, now they reach out globally. This ushers in new sexual, relational, and family configurations. Dating and being sexual with individuals from diverse locations builds new relational trajectories. Dating and relationshipping are no longer linear. The historic trajectory of first dating, then partnership and commitment, followed by a move in, has changed. The goal of long-term commitment or partnered residencing is not such a strong expectation. Relationships no longer need to be "going somewhere," with the goal of all life, sex, work, and relationships geared solely toward partnership, which is limiting, constraining, and future-oriented. This new sexual-relational ethic is based on an unbound intimacy that allows for the needed flexibility and temporariness of commitments that current economic life requires, along with increasing desire for autonomy and mobility untethered by permanent ties (Bernstein, 2007, p. 175).

New sexual-relational trajectories and norms are being established. Non-linear dating and singledom, where couples are learning that healthy relationships don't break up but instead change boundaries and often leave room for a return to romance and sexuality at a later time , are becoming more common. Deciding that a sexual-romantic or exclusively monogamous relational style is no longer desired does not have to lead to a complete end to all relating. Moving into a sex-only or friendship-only style is always an option. The archaic version of dating with long-term expectations has healthily been reduced to dating for the sake of experience, sexuality, and relationship. From the new model of "no breakups," dating and sex are used as forms of socialization and friendship creation.

Dating is seen as an expansion and not a reduction of a social life. There are now date nights for the couple, friend nights for non-romantic others, and solo nights for individual activities and interests. In addition, this lack of pervasive and obsessive prioritizing also allows for partners to be friends and not each other's salvation. "If partners could give each other the courtesies and space they give their friends, they wouldn't be so tense or resentful… We don't usually expect friends to fill mutual infantile needs" (Carter & Peters, 1996, p. 96). But the larger reality is that adults don't have needs, they have wants. When we are single, we get all our "needs" met, so partnerships should model more of a friendship style. "Stop picturing interactions between infants and mothers as the appropriate model for adult love relationships. Forget the idea that unmet 'attachment needs' are the primary source of your problems" (Schnarch, 2009, p. 85).

The new non-cohabitating partnership and marriage excludes spending every day, all day, together, under the same roof. Under the old model, "we become too familiar, take one another for granted… Domestic situations in themselves have a huge capacity to bring up buried emotions, and when these feelings come up, they're often more than a couple is prepared to handle" (Kingma, 1998, p. 37). Not cohabitating allows for needed space and processing, without the unnecessary tensions and too tight containment of living together, daily, under the same roof, with no space.

LIBERATED STAGES OF SEXUAL DEVELOPMENT

Webcam sexuality, where viewers watch each other, builds sexual self-esteem and body esteem through the erotic mirroring and validation from a diversity of others. This sexual confidence and community-building is vastly important for non-normative body types and sexual desires. The "globalized body" allows for identification and normalization of *all* and *any* bodies. Technology bridges everyone, creating available community for everything and anything sexual. The Internet can often be the only safe space for sexual expression, exploration, and socializing due to the policing of non-normativity in society. "For adolescents, this allows for the relational development they need to fall in and out of love with people and ideas. Real life does not always provide this kind of space, but the Internet does" (Turkle, 2011, p. 152), which is crucial for the identity and sexual creativity. It also aids adults, who likewise have missed out on the necessity of sexual-relational experiences for building confidence.

The typical undervaluing of non-normative relational configurations shows up here. Not all relationships need to be face-to-face, or include daily interaction in real time. In our busy and globalized culture, our relational forms need to meet our needs, and not have us believing we need to force ourselves into traditional standards.

Examples of new liberated relational styles include:

- online only
- serial marriage
- cross-generational
- plural (more than one partner)
- asexual (friendship-based, between friends)
- solo (non-partnered)
- open
- queer (no structure, no rules, fluid)

CYBORG BODY

New cyborg bodies will lead to new genders, sexes, and sexualities. "Cyborgs are the dominant social and cultural formations that are active throughout the social fabric...the Vitruvian Man has gone cybernetic" (Braidotti, 2013, p. 90). "The erotics of cyborgs promises the actual bionic construction of many sexualities and sexes. With transsexual surgery, complicated mechanical sexual aids, and the virtual magic of teledildonics, sexual identity is more plastic than it has ever been" (Gray, 2002, p. 158).

Anatomy is *not* destiny, it is only a starting point for further development and diversity. The term "transbiological" (Halberstam, 2008, p. 266) refers to how technology reconceptualizes the body. "For many people deemed disabled, in the world of technoscience their relationship with non-human actants has been profoundly cyborgical and hybridisable (for example the use of communication and adaptive devices, implants and transplants). As such the networks of association between human [and] non-human (sentient beings and machines) have always been and increasingly are pushing the boundaries" (Campbell, 2009, p. 7). The sexual future brings "experimentations with the boundaries of perfectibility of the body" and "moral panic about the disruption of centuries-old beliefs about human 'nature'" (Braidotti, 2013, p. 2). The limits of our sexual bodies will be endless, and the distance between the posthuman body and ideals of "nature" will be great.

DEATH OF THE FAMILY

The idealized form of "family" combined with a lack of vision for alternative options and styles of family has left many with the only option of assimilation into the current model. "It is often asserted that the heterosexual nuclear family is the basis for every human society. But this cozy domestic universalism simply is not supported by the evidence from cultural anthropology and social history" (Lancaster, 2003, p. 180). "The postmodern family condition is not a new model of family life equivalent to that of the modern family, and it is not the next step in an orderly progression of stages of family history; rather the postmodern family condition signals the moment in that history when our belief in logical progression of stages breaks down" (Stacey, 1996, p. 8). As new family forms—single parents, same-gender parents, multiple parents, and blended families—all gain support and show the health and sustainability of their configurations, these will soon become legitimate options for all.

"The relationships that emerge when families collapse and re-form also have value. They also nourish and expand us... They, too, bring all the gifts and lessons of relationships" (Kingma, 1998, p. 156). The world's largest study of same-sex parenting found that "there was no statistical difference between children of same-sex couples and the rest of the population on indicators including self-esteem, emotional behaviour and the amount of time spent with parents. However, children of same-sex couples scored higher than the national average for overall health and family cohesion, measuring how well a family gets along" (Ford, 2013).

"Two-parent families only make sense as a practical necessity if children are born into families isolated from larger community networks. That is, if it is possible for children to be exposed to and interact with a diverse array of human beings as they are nurtured to adulthood, the theoretical justifications generally put forth for needing two-parent homes lose their power" (Lehr, 1999, p. 110).

"Family" is a socially defined term and therefore is malleable. Institutional issues are not resolved just because of an extension of rights. Many diversely identified individuals are creating multiple family forms. True freedom is when all people are free to decide on their own chosen form of family without interference. Allowing same-sex marriage is a forward move, but it still creates exclusivity to one idea of family and ignores all the rest. "It is worth questioning whether the values that guided family understanding are now appropriate as a model of family life... These family values are embedded in maintaining a social organization that privileges a few" (Lehr, 1999, p. 45).

PARENTING WITHOUT GENDER AND CONTROL

Abandoning the constructs of gender leaves us with a non-segregated childhood and lifestyle. Far too much distance and separation is utilized between people of what are wrongly called opposite sexes. The experience of gender neutrality equates to allowing the wearing, purchasing, and experience of clothes and toys that a child or adolescent enjoys, regardless of their traditional arbitrary designations of "for girls or boys only." This is the loss of gender-coded boundaries that dictate what clothing can be worn and what activities an individual can engage in. Parenting that utilizes child-rearing strategies that focus on gender training in childhood is an early form of discrimination; it's a family style boot camp that sets in motion sexism and oppression for later adulthood. Allowing more behavioral options and choices is more robust for a child's development and parental relationship. This leads to the diversity that we all embody as we are all a blend of all gender traits and stereotypes. We do not need to force boys into men or girls into women; we need to raise children into adults. Allow children and individuals to self-identify and to choose without gendered limits their behaviors, toys, and clothes.

Male "mothers" (maternal manhood) and female "fathers" (paternal womanhood) and co-parenting versus mother/father roles provide all that a family or child requires. Parenting is about a relationship of care, not oppressive gender rules or behaviors. Good parenting is about the relationship you have with your children, and it is lifelong. It's the concept of fathering against fatherhood and mothering against motherhood, which is caretaking in ways that challenge norms and expectations. Parents living and parenting within stereotypes opposite of their gender dispel gender-based modes of behavior and the damaging myth that men and women are opposites.

Many cultural problems also stem from our standard parenting style, which is rooted in separation and obsessive individualism. Parents and children need closeness and identification, not separation and estrangement, for health and sustainability.

"Relational parenting" means not disconnecting from a child but instead prioritizing your relationship, as we are all less healthy when we live autonomously and try to stand alone on our own. Stay emotionally close as relationships, especially parenting, should not be about distance, independence, or punishment. When parents utilize a collaborative relational approach this trains a child to see parents and other relationships as enhancing and available for support. The traditional style of parenting from a perspective of control creates a tension that leads to children needing to separate and "break free" to feel empowered. This does not support an adult relational style where partners are seen as allies. Many parents treat sex as a problem to solve and a site for conflict that leads to distance with their children. When parents use a "relational" parenting model versus a traditional "separation" model to parent, they cultivate in their children and in themselves the skills and resources so they can remain close, allowing for training and internalization of a more relational model for life.

New Rules for Parenting:

1. Accept and normalize adolescent sexuality.
2. Stay connected and relational. Adolescence does not need to be about separation and autonomy.
3. Don't see sex as a problem to fix or prevent. It's a normal and expected stage of development.

4. Stop perpetuating the problematic idea of a gendered sexual battle where male sexuality is about perpetrating and stealing sex from females, thereby making female sexuality one of victimization. Females have sexual interest and sexual desire, and do want non-relational hookups. They are not just receptive and submissive.

SINGLEDOM AS ACCEPTABLE ENDPOINT

The brilliance of marginal and minority communities rests in the ability to ignore institutional norms and to lead a truly queer alternative lifestyle. An assimilationist mentality in terms of sexual-relational decision-making limits both the ability to make individual authentic choices and room for expansion. Attempts to direct one's sexual-relational life toward a pre-chosen social vision of relational health allows too much room for a hierarchical division of right versus wrong. The resultant shame has a toxic effect upon one's psychological fitness and health.

Traditional communities and sexual majorities have created a "developmental trajectory" that marginal communities have sadly and needlessly internalized to determine their own trajectories. "Straight" culture has co-opted the idea of growing "up," whereas queerer communities have abilities to allow for growing sideways.

There is a burden with the concept of age and all the socially constructed assumptions that parasitically attach themselves to notions of what an individual should be doing at their age. Society and psychology have an obsession with psychosocial stages of development and their related expectations and norms. There are typical patterns of social maturation and development, but subcultural evolution outside this trajectory is far from problematic and pathological. Examination of subcultures reveals diverse and non-normative expressions of socialization.

Many have seen the facial acknowledgment of normative peers when one discusses their chosen singledom, often seen as a sin due to the lack of a family-oriented lifestyle of no marriage or children. Some cannot fathom a lifestyle, identity, and social world built solely on career and pleasure-based attributes. A life centered around dating, work, and socializing can be treated as lacking and possibly immature. But maturity is subjective and built from the health of an individuated and consciously chosen life. There is a culturally enforced idea that in order to be an adult one must marry and have a family.

> People are not considered an adult until they marry… This means that if you are part of the queer community, you are perpetually a child, denied access to not only the social institutions that allow you to become an "adult," but also to all the cultural privileges and community support that come with getting married. People who live on the margins—whether we're talking about single women or queer couples—are accused of living irresponsible and/or immoral lives, and are often characterized as having made a "choice" to not grow up. (Mukhopadhyay, 2011, p. 55)

My career has definitely shown me heinous examples of lives chosen by others and by norms and false demonstrations of maturity. Being single, career-centered, or socially driven is not regressive, primitive, or irresponsible. The oxymoronic error of calling any modern-day behavior regressive is an impossibility, as we cannot literally regress. We can only mimic prior behavior, but it still emerges from a current-day adult. And most non-normative behavior is an act of confidence and health. Healthy people choose their own trajectories and distinct lifestyles.

"*The family* is a peculiarly Western and modern concept. Some cultures do not employ the category of 'family' at all. Many societies that do use the term do so to depict diverse relationships and to convey diverse meanings" (Stacey, 1996, p. 38). Not all cultures choose to involve the tension of nuclear family versus outer social world. I see multitudes of urban couples who have chosen to have children and yet maintain full social lives distinct from their family lives. I witness far too many modernist attacks on those who do not place certain aspects at the center of their lives. We all get to choose our relational priorities, and anything short of that is an oppressive form of social policing. I've sat through far too many case consults listening to therapists proselytizing about the importance and primacy of the family. That is not a psychologically sound concept but instead a moral value judgment. Psychology has no room for this subjective, externally referented mind control. A true liberation-centered individual lives on a trajectory that is self-directed and self-chosen.

The future will be a deconstruction of relational expectations and trajectories. We now have one of the highest rates of singledom, and having examined some of its causes, especially the flaws with the current structure of marriage and monogamy, it's important to distinguish being without romantic coupling as an appropriate and legitimate relational style and choice. Traditionally the expectation has been to start out relationally uncoupled, then work to find a partner. The endpoint and finish line has always been being coupled. But the reality is that the trajectory should be circular and not a straight line with an endpoint. Relationships have new parameters and "standards that don't include 'Where is this going?' but rather 'Is this a nice person and is this relationship stable?'" (Mukhopadhyay, 2011, p. 30).

Moving in and out of relationships, with periods of coupling and uncoupling, is both the new standard and a healthy process. We learn about ourselves and others while in a relationship, and longevity is not always available or desired. This is far from a failure. Relationships cannot be a failure, as they have no goal. They are a process, an active system that we enter and engage with. Relationships ending should come with no surprise or sadness, but instead a shift into a new relational style. No breakups but instead new boundaries. From a romantic sexual style to a platonic social one. The options are far greater than just coupled or single. There are hundreds of interesting and healthy options and configurations that fall between these two choices. Some of these may involve sex and some may not.

Relationships serve many purposes and are one of the key factors in what creates the happiest people. But the studies highlight that it is relationships and not marriage or romantic coupling that is needed. The fundamental point is that if we further the maxim that a happy life necessitates finding a partner, this panic will breed both misery and a continuation of anti-single support. "Households with married couples are in the minority, with the majority of Americans living single. Americans will spend more of their lives single than married" (DePaulo, 2006, p. 7). And yet, singledom continues to be looked down upon as unfinished, on its way toward coupling, or unhealthy.

NO IDEALS

Relationships are all diverse and created based on those within the system. Have no relational ideals, as these are all inherited. And our historical understandings of what love and dating should look like have all been anti-woman and repressive. Even within the mental health field, many archaic and anxious therapists project their own lack of relational health and comfort with diversity onto their clients, trapping them in models and ideals that are oppressive, limited, and a lie.

Throw out the vision you have of "how it should be," because this keeps you trapped in a fantasy. Instead allow your love, sexuality, and relational life to take on alternative and creative frameworks, meanings, configurations, and trajectories. As a therapist herself says,

> My own relationships broke the rules of convention and assumed surprising and extraordinary forms… Everyone I was counseling was also living in relationships that were in conflict with their own definitions of what a relationship should be…taking on forms that shocked them… These startling new relationships, which conventional minds might call aberrant, are actually Roman candles lighting the way to a world of new possibility… There's nothing the matter with any of us, but there is a grand transformation… Love is the wrecking ball that is pulverizing every relationship of record that isn't wide enough or brave enough to let real love in. (Kingma, 1998, p. 5–6)

THE NEW RULES FOR DATING

1. Dating is done for the sake of experiencing others, interpersonal growth, diverse sex, and building new relationships and friends for life. Dating is not done for the sole purpose of making a long-term romantic commitment.
2. Dating is a phase of multiplicity. It is not an instant commitment. Date many people at one time to grow, build diverse experiences, and decide if you want a committed, exclusive relationship with anyone. Instant monogamy or commitment are not a part of dating. They occur as an end result, if at all.

3. Dating is not a promise of anything other than today. Dating says, "I am with you right now, for the sake of fun today, and I am not committing or promising that I will want more or to continue to relate to you romantically tomorrow."
4. Date only if you are happy. If not, you will try to use your partner to make you happy; that is not their job. It's relational misuse. Go build a life that makes you happy so that you are a solid and developed self for another to date. Unhappy people should be wrapped in police tape, as they are unsafe and not ready to be dated.
5. Date only if you have a solid group of good friends. If not, you will misuse your partner as your sole social outlet. Healthy others will buckle under the weight of the expectations of being everything to you. It is appropriate and required to have many others to share and experience life with. People with limited relationships (of all categories) are limited in development. If you do not have the skills required for making and maintaining friendships, you definitely do not have the skills required for dating.
6. Date up. Date people who make you nervous because they are healthier than you. Date people who speak to your best and do not relate to you from your worst. Most people choose partners from their worst and most anxious. This says, "I feel comfortable with you because you will let me act out my shit, and I will let you act out yours."
7. Date as yourself. From date number one, embody all your many selves. Do not present and perform as the person you think your other would like, to then surprise attack them with your many selves later in the relationship.
8. Dating is a process of hurting and being hurt. This process will engender a lot of disappointment and

frustration. If you are not ready to disappoint another person, then you are not ready to date.

9. Have sex sooner rather than later. Sexuality is the most important level of intimacy and compatibility, and the way we can learn the most about another person, so do not delay this learning experience. Connections on other levels do *not* promise a sexual connection.
10. Healthy people do not have breakups. They leave the romantic relationship with care, and work to maintain friendships with their exes. People who are not friends with any of their exes are showing you your fate with them when things end. You too will be left dramatically and disparaged when the relationship is over. You can tell the health of an other by asking if they are friends with their exes and how their last relationship ended.
11. There are no rules. Ignore any set of rules your friends, magazines, or dating coach have told you. These are gimmicks. If you like someone, be vulnerable and show them. People who are truly interested in you are happy when you also act interested in them.
12. Get online. Online dating and sex are the new methods.
13. Marriage is *not* always the goal *or* the best relationship form. *Have no* standardized relational form.

EPILOGUE

The work and journey toward living "sex outside the lines" requires a new awareness of the self in the world. Our culture and all of its institutions work against the liberation you value and need. Our work involves examining what beliefs and ways of being we are feeding, as our sexual reality is built and determined by the choices we make, how we talk about sex, how we have sex, and with whom we are sexual. Ending erotophobia (abstinence-only sex education, silencing sexual language, anti-porn discourse, sex addiction theory and treatment, heteronormative psychologies, limited identity politics, gender norms, etc.) is about dismantling all forms of hierarchical social oppression (including its intersection with race, class, age, and mental and physical abilities). "Sexual minorities [like *all* minorities] share a history of injustice: [all] have been pathologized by medicine; demonized by religion; discriminated against in housing, employment, and education; stereotyped in representation; victimized by hate groups; [and] isolated socially" (Sandahl, 2003, p. 26). Sex outside the lines looks like living in the world without adherence to norms, challenging mental health diagnostics, being fluid and multiphrenic with identity, creating new ways of relating, valuing all sex as legitimate, and challenging and limiting institutions and discourses that devalue and shame sex and its liberation.

All this inherently creates the need for social-sexual activism, as it deconstructs the typical anti-sex language and ways of being. Sexual imagination is needed to then push the boundaries of sexual reality and aid us in transgressing the norms the dominant culture has forced upon us. Sexual imagination removes the shackles of imposed social limits and the sexual colonization of the mind, and it leaves us in a tension against ourselves. "Our limits are the ones that we know are set by ourselves, so passing beyond (transgressing) them can only mean rebelling against ourselves" (Gutting, 2005, p. 17). Once the sexual liberatory work has been completed, we are left with only ourselves to battle and transgress. Sexual health means removing external bounds and replacing them with an internal struggle for what's right for *you* based on *your* chosen integrity and values.

Sex outside the lines means "being aware that there is something unsatisfying and dishonest about the way sex is talked about (or hidden) in [our] daily life. It also means questioning the ways our society assigns privilege based on adherence to its moral codes, and in fact makes every sexual choice a matter of morality. If you believe that these [inequalities] can be addressed only through extreme social change, then you" are sexually liberated (Califia, 2000, p. xii). A sexually healthy consciousness resists containment and labeling, and imagines more expansion and creativity.

ACKNOWLEDGMENTS

My best friend taught me that owning the "work" is not as important as being part of the "work," and that many people are involved in this process. Following this, I want to honor those who are also doing the work of sexual liberation and health, and have motivated, inspired, and supported me in my mission.

Hours and hours of writing, theorizing, processing, and therapitizing with Conner Habib has propelled me forward, kept me radical, and also helped me learn about my own work and sexual self, all intersecting and developing this book. His love and guidance continue to make me evolve and blow my mind!

Kate Russel, all the way back from high school, sat on my couch for many hours helping me construct an amazing book proposal, and for many more hours of Aunt Viv, laughing indecently, and being sartorial. Your support also moves me.

Thanks to Dewayne Jones, who was with me at the very beginning of all this "Dr. Donaghue" stuff and always believed in my abilities. You are woven into all of this.

My book agent, Jeff Silberman, who held my hand and kicked my ass through the book manuscript process, and kept me from giving up when it got tough, was always a support when I got lost or "too '60s free love."

Thank you to Glenn and everyone at BenBella for taking on this project and working tirelessly to get the message out there.

Thank you, Erin, for helping to make my neologisms and ideas more digestible and readable. I can only imagine what it felt like to be buried under all my ramblings. You gave my work respect and more power.

To the front-line sexual radicals, sex workers, and sexual liberators, whose very lives are activism, and who show that even in the face of sex-hating law, medicine, and psychology, you will continue to push forward with your integrity and not allow phobic norms to guide you. You all inspire me!

Most importantly, to my family, who always loved this tattooed, manic insurgent and found value in all I did. Your continued interest and support in all I do has allowed the safety net needed to "jump off the cliff" and go all the way. Let this book also honor Dad, who kept us all together and was always the rock we needed him to be. He was always my biggest fan.

ABOUT THE AUTHOR

Dr. Chris Donaghue is a doctor of clinical sexology and human sexuality, trained doctorally in clinical psychology, a licensed clinical therapist, and a certified sex therapist.

He specializes in individual and couples sex and marital therapy with a private practice in Los Angeles, California.

Dr. Donaghue is nationally recognized as a sex and relationship expert, having been featured in *Newsweek*, CNN, OWN, HLN, and *National Geographic*.

He is co-host of WE tv's *Sex Box*.

REFERENCES

Abramson, P. *Sex Appeal: Six Ethical Principles for the 21st Century*. New York: Oxford University Press, 2010.

Alaimo, S. "Eluding Capture: The Science, Culture, and Pleasure of 'Queer' Animals" in *Queer Ecologies: Sex, Nature, Politics, Desire*, C. Mortimer-Sandilands and B. Erickson, eds. Bloomington: Indiana University Press, 2010.

Altman, D. *Homosexual: Oppression and Liberation*. New York: New York University Press, 1993.

Apple, M. *Ideology and the Curriculum*. New York: Routledge, 1990.

Bagemihl, B. *Biological Exuberance: Animal Homosexuality and Natural Diversity*. New York: St. Martin's Press, 1999.

Barcan, R. *Nudity: A Cultural Anatomy*. Oxford: Berg, 2004.

Barker, C., and S. Murray. "Disabling Postcolonialism: Global Disability Cultures and Democratic Criticism" in *The Disability Studies Reader*, 4th ed., L. Davis, ed. New York and London: Routledge, 2013.

Barnett, R., and C. Rivers. *Same Difference: How Gender Myths Are Hurting Our Relationships, Our Children, and Our Jobs*. New York: Basic Books, 2004.

Baudrillard, J. "The Final Solution: Cloning Beyond the Human and Inhuman" in *The Vital Illusion*, J. Witwer, ed. New York: Columbia University Press, 2001.

Becker, H. S. *Outsiders: Studies in the Sociology of Deviance*. New York: Free Press, 1963.

Ben-Ze'ev, A. *Love Online: Emotions on the Internet*. New York and Cambridge, UK: Cambridge University Press, 2004.

Bergman, S. *Men's Psychological Development: A Relational Perspective*. Work in Progress (Stone Center for Developmental Services and Studies). Wellesley Center for Women. Paper no. 48. 1991.

Bergstrand, C., and J. Sinski. *Swinging in America: Love, Sex, and Marriage in the 21st Century*. Santa Barbara, CA: Praeger, 2010.

Bernauer, J. "Michel Foucault's Ecstatic Thinking" in *The Final Foucault*, J. Bernauer and D. Rasmussen, eds. Cambridge, MA: MIT Press, 1988.

Bersani, L. *Is the Rectum A Grave?: And Other Essays*. Chicago: University of Chicago Press, 2010.

Bersani, L., and A. Phillips. *Intimacies*. Chicago: The University of Chicago Press, 2008.

Bernstein, E. *Temporarily Yours: Intimacy, Authenticity, and the Commerce of Sex*. Chicago and London: The University of Chicago Press, 2007.

Birden, S. *Rethinking Sexual Identity in Education*. Lanham, MD: Rowman & Littlefield Publishers, 2005.

Birnbaum, G., M. Mikulincer, H. Reis, A. Orpaz, and O. Gillath. "When Sex Is More Than Just Sex: Attachment Orientations, Sexual Experience, and Relationship Quality." *Journal of Personality and Social Psychology* 91, no. 5 (2006): 929–943.

Blank, H. *Straight: The Surprisingly Short History of Heterosexuality*. Boston: Beacon Press, 2012.

Bordo, S. *The Male Body: A New Look at Men in Public and in Private*. New York: Farrar, Straus and Giroux, 1999.

———. *Unbearable Weight: Feminism, Western Culture, and the Body*. Berkeley: University of California Press, 2003.

Braidotti, R. *Nomadic Subjects: Embodiment and Sexual Difference in Contemporary Feminist Theory*. New York: Columbia University Press, 2011.

———. *The Posthuman*. Cambridge, UK: Polity Press, 2013.

Brown, W. *States of Injury: Power and Freedom in Late Modernity*. Princeton, NJ: Princeton University Press, 1995.

Bruhm, S., and N. Hurley. *Curiouser: On the Queerness of Children*. Minneapolis: University of Minnesota Press, 2004.

Buchbinder, D. *Studying Men and Masculinities*. New York: Routledge, 2013.

Burman, E. *Deconstructing Developmental Psychology*, 2nd ed. New York: Routledge Press, 2008.

Butler, J. *Gender Trouble: Feminism and the Subversion of Identity*. London: Routledge, 1990.

———. "Imitation and Gender Insubordination" in *Inside/Out: Lesbian Theories, Gay Theories*, D. Fuss, ed. New York: Routledge, 1991.

Califia, P. *Public Sex: The Culture of Radical Sex*. San Francisco: Cleis Press, 2000.

Campbell, F. *Contours of Ableism: The Production of Disability and Abledness*. New York: Palgrave Macmillan, 2009.

Carter, E., and J. Peters. *Love, Honor & Negotiate: Building Partnerships That Last a Lifetime*. New York: Pocket Books, 1996.

Cavanagh, S. *Sexing the Teacher: School Sex Scandals and Queer Pedagogies*. Vancouver: UBC Press, 2007.

Clancy, S. *The Trauma Myth: The Truth about the Sexual Abuse of Children—and Its Aftermath*. New York: Basic Books, 2009.

Clare, E. "Gawking, Gaping, Staring" in "Desiring Disability: Queer Theory Meets Disability Studies," R. McRuer and A. Wilkerson, eds., special issue, *Journal of Lesbian and Gay Studies* 9, no. 1/2 (2003): 257–261.

Clulow, C., ed. *Sex, Attachment, and Couple Psychotherapy: Psychoanalytic Perspectives*. London: Karnac, 2009.

Contratto, S. "A Feminist Critique of Attachment Theory and Evolutionary Psychology" in *Rethinking Mental Health and Disorder,* M. Ballou and L. Brown, eds. New York: The Guilford Press, 2002.

Coyne, J. "The Fairy Tales of Evolutionary Psychology: Of Vice and Men." *The New Republic*, April 3, 2000, 27–34.

Cozolino, L. *The Neuroscience of Human Relationships: Attachment and the Developing Social Brain*. New York: W.W. Norton & Company, 2006.

Curra, J. *The Relativity of Deviance*. Thousand Oaks, CA: Sage Publications, 2000.

Cvetkovich, A. *An Archive of Feelings: Trauma, Sexuality and Lesbian Public Cultures*. Durham, NC: Duke University Press, 2003.

D'Amato, A. "Porn Up, Rape Down." Northwestern Public Law Research Paper No. 913013, Northwestern University School of Law, Chicago, IL, June 23, 2006. http://dx.doi.org/10.2139/ssrn.913013

Davis, A. *The Meaning of Freedom: And Other Difficult Dialogues*. San Francisco: City Lights Books, 2012.

Davis, J. E. "Forbidden Fruit: Black Males' Constructions of Transgressive Sexualities in Middle School" in *Queering Elementary Education: Advancing the Dialogue about Sexualities and Schooling*, W. Letts and J. Sears, eds. Lanham, MD: Rowman & Littlefield Publishers, 1999.

Davis, L. "The End of Identity Politics and the Beginning of Dismodernism: On Disability as an Unstable Category" in *The Disability Studies Reader*, 4th ed., L. Davis, ed. New York and London: Routledge, 2013a.

———. *The End of Normal: Identity in a Biocultural Era*. Ann Arbor: University of Michigan Press, 2013b.

Dean, T. *Beyond Sexuality*. Chicago: University of Chicago Press, 2000.

———. *Unlimited Intimacy: Reflections on the Subculture of Barebacking*. Chicago: University of Chicago Press, 2009.

Dean, T., and C. Lane, eds. *Homosexuality & Psychoanalysis*. Chicago and London: University of Chicago Press, 2001.

DePaulo, B. *Singled Out: How Singles Are Stereotyped, Stigmatized, and Ignored, and Still Live Happily Ever After*. New York: St. Martin's Press, 2006.

Diamond, M. "The Effects of Pornography: An International Perspective" in *Porn 101: Eroticism, Pornography, and the First Amendment*, J. Elias, V. Elias, V. Bullough, and G. Brewer, eds. Amherst, NY: Prometheus Press, 1999.

———. "Pornography, Public Acceptance and Sex Related Crime: A Review." *International Journal of Law and Psychiatry* 32, no. 5 (2009): 304–314.

Dill, K. *How Fantasy Becomes Reality: Seeing Through Media Influence*. New York: Oxford University Press, 2009.

Dimen, M. *Sexuality, Intimacy, Power*. Hillsdale, NJ: The Analytic Press, 2003.

Dodson, B. *Orgasms for Two: The Joy of Partnersex*. New York: Harmony Books, 2002.

———. *Sex for One: The Joy of Selfloving*. New York: Three Rivers Press, 1996.

Doi, T. *The Anatomy of Dependence: The Key Analysis of Japanese Behavior*. New York: Kodansha, 2014.

Doidge, N. *The Brain That Changes Itself: Stories of Personal Triumph from the Frontiers of Brain Science*. New York: Penguin Books, 2007.

Dollimore, J. "Sexual Disgust" in *Homosexuality & Psychoanalysis*, T. Dean and C. Lane, eds. Chicago and London: University of Chicago Press, 2001.

———. *Sexual Dissidence: Augustine to Wilde, Freud to Foucault*. Oxford: Clarendon Press, 1991.

Domenici, T., and R. Lesser, eds. *Disorienting Sexuality: Psychoanalytic Reappraisals of Sexual Identities*. New York: Routledge Press, 1995.

Dudley-Marling, C., and A. Gurn. *The Myth of the Normal Curve*. New York: Peter Lang, 2010.

Duggan, L. "The New Homonormativity: The Sexual Politics of Neoliberalism" in *Materializing Democracy: Toward a Revitalized Cultural Politics*, R. Castronovo and D. Nelson, eds. Durham, NC: Duke University Press, 2002.

Dutton, K. *The Wisdom of Psychopaths: What Saints, Spies, and Serial Killers Can Teach Us about Success*. New York: Scientific American/Farrar, Straus and Giroux, 2012.

Easton, D., and J. Hardy. *The Ethical Slut: A Practical Guide to Polyamory, Open Relationships & Other Adventures*. Berkeley: Celestial Arts, 2009.

Eckert, L. "Post(-)Anarchism and the *Contrasexual* Practices of *Cyborgs* in *Dildotopia*" in *Anarchism and Sexuality: Ethics, Relationships, and Power*, J. Heckert and R. Cleminson, eds. London and New York: Routledge, 2011.

Edelman, L. *No Future: Queer Theory and Death Drive*. Durham, NC: Duke University Press, 2004.

Egan, R. *Becoming Sexual: A Critical Appraisal of the Sexualization of Girls*. Cambridge, UK: Polity Press, 2013.

Ehrenberg, M., and O. Ehrenberg. *The Intimate Circle: The Sexual Dynamics of Family Life*. New York: Simon & Schuster, 1988.

Ehrensaft, D. *Gender Born, Gender Made: Raising Healthy Gender-Nonconforming Children*. New York: Experiment, 2011.

Ellis, A. *Sex without Guilt in the 21st Century*. Fort Lee, NJ: Barricade Books, 2003.

Emens, E. "Disabling Attitudes: U.S. Disability Law and the ADA Amendments Act" in *The Disability Studies Reader*, 4th ed., L. Davis, ed. New York and London: Routledge, 2013.

Epstein, D., and R. Johnson. *Schooling Sexualities*. Buckingham, UK: Open University Press, 1998.

Epstein, D., and J. Sears. *A Dangerous Knowing: Sexuality, Pedagogy, and Popular Culture*. New York: Cassell, 1999.

Epstein, R., ed. *Who's Your Daddy?: And Other Writings on Queer Parenting*. Toronto: Sumach Press, 2009.

Erickson, L. "Out of Line: The Sexy Femmegimp Politics of Flaunting It!" in *The Feminist Porn Book: The Politics of Producing Pleasure*, T. Taormino, C. Shimizu, C. Penley, and M. Miller-Young, eds. New York: The Feminist Press, 2012.

Evans, J. "A Queer Spawn Manifesto: Empowerment and Recognition" in *Who's Your Daddy?: And Other Writings on Queer Parenting,* R. Epstein, ed. Toronto: Sumach Press, 2009.

Farber, S. *The Spiritual Gift of Madness: The Failure of Psychiatry and the Rise of the Mad Pride Movement*. Rochester, VT: Inner Traditions, 2012.

Farrell, W. *The Myth of Male Power: Why Men Are the Disposable Sex*. New York: Berkley Books, 1993.

Fausto-Sterling, A. *Sexing the Body: Gender Politics and the Construction of Sexuality*. New York: Basic Books, 2000.

Fine, C. *Delusions of Gender: How Our Minds, Society, and Neurosexism Create Differences*. New York: W.W. Norton & Company, 2010.

Fine, M. "Sexuality, Schooling, and Adolescent Females: The Missing Discourse of Desire." *Harvard Educational Review* 58, no. 1 (Spring 1988): 29–54.

Fischer, N. "Purity and Pollution: Sex as a Moral Discourse" in *Introducing the New Sexuality Studies*, 2nd ed., S. Seidman, N. Fischer, and C. Meeks, eds. New York: Routledge, 2011.

Fonagy, P. "Foreword" in *Sex, Attachment, and Couple Psychotherapy: Psychoanalytic Perspectives*, C. Clulow, ed. London: Karnac, 2009.

Ford, J., D. Mongon, and M. Whelan. *Special Education and Social Control: Invisible Disasters*. London: Routledge & Kegan Paul, 1982.

Ford, Z. "World's Largest Study of Same-Sex Parenting Finds That Children Are Thriving." ThinkProgress. June 5, 2013. http://thinkprogress.org/lgbt/2013/06/05/2106751/same-sex-parenting-study/. Retrieved January 5, 2015.

Foucault, M. *The Birth of the Clinic: An Archaeology of Medical Perception*. New York: Vintage, 1973.

———. *The History of Sexuality, Vol. 1: An Introduction*. New York: Vintage, 1978.

———. *Power/Knowledge: Selected Interviews and Other Writings, 1972–1977*, C. Gordon, ed. New York: Pantheon, 1980.

Fox, D., I. Prilleltensky, and S. Austin, eds. *Critical Psychology: An Introduction*, 2nd ed. Los Angeles, CA: Sage Publications, 2009.

Frances, A. *Saving Normal: An Insider's Revolt against Out-of-Control Psychiatric Diagnosis, DSM-5, Big Pharma, and the Medicalization of Ordinary Life*. New York: William Morrow, 2013.

Friedman, A. *Blind to Sameness: Sexpectations and the Social Construction of Male and Female Bodies*. Chicago: University of Chicago Press, 2013.

Friedman, J. *What You Really Really Want: The Smart Girl's Shame-Free Guide to Sex and Safety*. Berkeley: Seal Press, 2011.

Fromm, E. *Escape from Freedom*. New York: Henry Holt and Company, 1969.

Galician, G., and D. Merskin. *Critical Thinking About Sex, Love, and Romance in the Mass Media: Media Literacy Applications*. Mahwah, NJ: Lawrence Erlbaum Associates, 2007.

Gallop, J. *Feminist Accused of Sexual Harassment*. Durham, NC: Duke University Press, 1997.

Garland-Thomson, R. *Extraordinary Bodies: Figuring Physical Disability in American Culture and Literature*. New York: Columbia University Press, 1997.

Gelb, S. "Evolutionary Anxiety, Monstrosity, and the Birth of Normality" in *The Myth of the Normal Curve*, C. Dudley-Marling and A. Gurn, eds. New York: Peter Lang, 2010.

Gergen, K. "Multiple Identity: The Healthy, Happy Human Being Wears Many Masks" in *The Truth About the Truth: De-confusing and Re-constructing the Postmodern World*, W. Anderson, ed. New York: Jeremy P. Tarcher/Penguin, 1995.

Gherovici, P. *Please Select Your Gender: From the Invention of Hysteria to the Democratizing of Transgenderism*. New York: Routledge, 2010.

Giddens, A. *The Transformation of Intimacy: Sexuality, Love & Eroticism in Modern Societies*. Stanford, CA: Stanford University Press, 1992.

Giffney, N., and M. Hird. *Queering the Non/Human*. Burlington, VT: Ashgate Publishing, 2008.

Gilbert, J. "Between Sexuality and Narrative: On the Language of Sex Education" in *Youth and Sexualities: Pleasure, Subversion, and Insubordination in and out of Schools*, M. Rasmussen, E. Rofes, and S. Talburt, eds. New York: Palgrave Macmillan, 2004.

Gladwell, M. *Outliers: The Story of Success*. New York: Back Bay Books, 2008.

Glass, S. *Not "Just Friends": Rebuilding Trust and Recovering Your Sanity After Infidelity*. New York: Free Press, 2004.

Goldman, A. "Plain Sex" in *The Philosophy of Sex: Contemporary Readings*, 3rd ed., A. Soble, ed. Lanham, MD: Rowman and Littlefield Publishers, 1997.

Good, G. *Humanism Betrayed: Theory, Ideology, and Culture in the Contemporary University*. Montreal: McGill-Queen's University Press, 2001.

Gray, C. *Cyborg Citizen: Politics in the Posthuman Age*. New York: Routledge, 2002.

Green, A., ed. *Sexual Fields: Toward a Sociology of Collective Sexual Life*. Chicago: University of Chicago Press, 2014.

Green, D. "Is Separation Really So Great?" in *Diversity and Complexity in Feminist Therapy*, L. Brown and M. Root, eds. New York: Harrington Park Press, 1990.

Green R., "Variant Forms of Human Sexual Behavior" in *Reproduction in Mammals: Volume 8, Human Sexuality*, C. Austin and R. Short, eds., Cambridge, UK: Cambridge University Press, 1980.

Greenspan, M. *A New Approach to Women & Therapy*, 2nd ed. Blue Ridge Summit, PA: Tab Books, 1993.

Gutting, G. *Foucault: A Very Short Introduction*. Oxford: Oxford University Press, 2005.

Hakim, C. *The New Rules: Internet Dating, Playfairs, and Erotic Power*. London, UK: Gibson Square, 2012.

Halberstam, J. "Animating Revolt/Revolting Animation: Penguin Love, Doll Sex and the Spectacle of the Queer Nonhuman" in *Queering the Non/Human*, N. Giffney and M. Hird, eds. Burlington, VT: Ashgate Publishing, 2008.

Halperin, D. *How to Be Gay*. Cambridge, MA: The Belknap Press of Harvard University, 2012.

Halwani, R. *Virtuous Liaisons: Care, Love, Sex and Virtue Ethics*. Chicago: Open Court, 2003.

Haraway, D. *Simians, Cyborgs, and Women: The Reinvention of Nature*. New York: Routledge, 1991.

Harris, A. *Gender as Soft Assembly*. New York: Routledge, 2009.

Harvey, J., A. Wenzel, and S. Sprecher, eds. *The Handbook of Sexuality in Close Relationships*. Mahwah, NJ: Lawrence Erlbaum Associates, 2004.

Heckert, J. "Love without Borders? Intimacy, Identity, and the State of Compulsory Monogamy" in *Understanding Non-Monogamies*, M. Barker and D. Langdridge, eds. New York: Routledge Press, 2010.

Heins, M. *Not in Front of the Children: "Indecency," Censorship, and the Innocence of Youth*. New Brunswick, NJ: Rutgers University Press, 2007.

Herdt, G. *Guardians of the Flutes: Idioms of Masculinity*. Chicago: The University of Chicago Press, 1987.

Hillman, J. *The Soul's Code: In Search of Character and Calling*. New York: Warner Books, 1996.

———. *The Thought of the Heart and the Soul of the World*. New York: Spring Publications, 1992.

Hird, M. "Animal Trans" in *Queering the Non/Human*. N. Giffney and M. Hird, eds. Burlington, VT: Ashgate Publishing, 2008a.

———. "Queer(y)ing Intersex: Reflections on Counselling People with Intersex Conditions" in *Feeling Queer or Queer Feelings? Radical Approaches to Counselling Sex, Sexualities and Genders*, L. Moon, ed. London and New York: Routledge. 2008b.

———. *Sex, Gender and Science*. Basingstoke, UK: Palgrave, 2004.

Hodges, I. "Queer Dilemmas: The Problem of Power in Psychotherapeutic and Counselling Practice" in *Feeling Queer or Queer Feelings? Radical Approaches to Counselling Sex, Sexualities and Genders*, L. Moon, ed. London and New York: Routledge, 2008.

———. "Queerying Freud: On Using Psychoanalysis with Sexual Minority Clients" in *Counselling Ideologies: Queer Challenges to Heteronormativity*, L. Moon, ed. Farnham, UK: Ashgate, 2010.

Hook, D. *Foucault, Psychology, and the Analytics of Power*. New York: Palgrave Macmillan, 2007.

hooks, b. *Teaching to Transgress: Education as the Practice of Freedom*. New York: Routledge, 1994.

Horrocks, R. *Masculinity in Crisis: Myths, Fantasies, and Realities*. New York: St. Martin's Press, 1994.

Hubbard, R. *The Politics of Women's Biology*. New Brunswick, NJ: Rutgers University Press, 1990.

Hubbard, T., and B. Verstraete, eds. *Censoring Sex Research: The Debate over Male Intergenerational Relations*. Walnut Creek, CA: Left Coast Press, 2013.

Illich, I. *Deschooling Society*. New York: Marion Boyars, 1970.

———. *Limits to Medicine: Medical Nemesis, The Expropriation of Health*. New York: Marion Boyars, 1977.

Ingraham, C. *Thinking Straight: The Power, the Promise, and the Paradox of Heterosexuality*. New York: Routledge, 2005.

———. *White Weddings: Romancing Heterosexuality in Popular Culture*, 2nd ed. New York: Routledge, 2008.

Ingram, G., A. Bouthillette, and Y. Retter. *Queers in Space: Communities, Public Places, Sites of Resistance*. Seattle: Bay Press, 1997.

Irvine, J. *Disorders of Desire: Sex and Gender in Modern American Sexology*, 2nd ed. Philadelphia: Temple University Press, 2005.

James, K. "Sexual Pleasure" in *Introducing the New Sexuality Studies*, 2nd ed., S. Seidman, N. Fisher, and C. Meeks, eds. New York: Routledge, 2011.

Jennings, T. *An Ethic of Queer Sex: Principles and Improvisations*. Chicago: Exploration Press, 2013.

Johnson, R. "Contested Borders, Contingent Lives: An Introduction" in *Border Patrols: Policing the Boundaries of Heterosexuality*, D. Steinberg, D. Epstein, and R. Johnson, eds. London: Cassell, 1997.

Johnson, S. "Promoting Easy Sex Without Genuine Intimacy: *Maxim* and *Cosmopolitan* Cover Lines and Cover Images" in *Critical Thinking About Sex, Love, and Romance in the Mass Media: Media Literacy Applications*, G. Galician and D. Merskin, eds. Mahwah, NJ: Lawrence Erlbaum Associates, 2007.

Johnston, L., and R. Longhurst. *Space, Place, and Sex: Geographies of Sexualities*. Lanham, MD: Rowman & Littlefield Publishers, 2010.

Jones, A. "Desire, Sexual Harassment, and Pedagogy in the University Classroom." *Theory into Practice* 35, no. 2 (1996): 102–109.

Jordan, J. "Relational Awareness: Transforming Disconnection" in *The Complexity of Connection: Writings from the Stone Center's Jean Baker Miller Training Institute*, J. Jordan, M. Walker, and L. Hartling, eds. New York: The Guilford Press, 2004a.

———. "Relational Resilience" in *The Complexity of Connection: Writings from the Stone Center's Jean Baker Miller Training Institute*, J. Jordan, M. Walker, and L. Hartling, eds. New York: The Guilford Press, 2004b.

Jordan-Young, R. *Brain Storm: The Flaws in the Science of Sex Differences*. Cambridge, MA: Harvard University Press, 2010.

Jung, C. G. *The Undiscovered Self*. New York: Signet, 1957.

Jung, F. "'The Truth Is…'—Lesbian Narratives of Gender" in *Bound and Unbound: Interdisciplinary Approaches to Genders and Sexualities*, Z. Davy, L. Eckert, N. Gerodetti, D. Llinares, and A. C. Santos, eds. Newcastle, UK: Cambridge Scholars Publishing, 2008.

Kafer, A. *Feminist, Queer, Crip*. Bloomington: Indiana University Press, 2013.

Kahr, B. *Who's Been Sleeping in Your Head?: The Secret World of Sexual Fantasies*. New York: Basic Books, 2008.

Kaplan, D. "Sexual Liberation and the Creative Class in Israel" in *Introducing the New Sexuality Studies*, 2nd ed., S. Seidman, N. Fischer, and C. Meeks, eds. New York: Routledge, 2011.

Katz, J. N. *The Invention of Heterosexuality*. New York: Penguin, 1996.

Kellner, D. "Cultural Studies, Multiculturalism, and Media Culture" in *Gender, Race, and Class in Media*, G. Dines and J. Humez, eds. Thousand Oaks, CA: Sage Publications, 1994.

Kimmel, M. S., and A. Linders. "Does Censorship Make a Difference? An Aggregate Empirical Analysis of Pornography and Rape." *Journal of Psychology & Human Sexuality* 8, no. 3 (1996): 1–20.

Kingma, D. *The Future of Love: The Power of the Soul in Intimate Relationships*. New York: Doubleday, 1998.

Kinsey, A. *Sexual Behavior in the Human Male*. Philadelphia: W. B. Saunders Co., 1948.

Kipnis, L. *Against Love: A Polemic*. New York: Vintage Books, 2003.

———. *Bound and Gagged: Pornography and the Politics of Fantasy in America*. Durham, NC: Duke University Press, 2007.

Kleinman, A. *Rethinking Psychiatry: From Cultural Category to Personal Experience*. New York: Free Press, 1988.

Kleinplatz, P. *New Directions in Sex Therapy: Innovations and Alternatives*. New York: Routledge, 2012.

Kolb, B., R. Gibb, and T. Robinson. "Brain Plasticity and Behavior." *Current Directions in Psychological Science* 12, no. 1 (2003): 1–5.

Kramer, L. "Gay Culture, Redefined." *New York Times*, December 12, 1997, A23.

Kumashiro, K. "Reading Queer Asian American Masculinities and Sexualities in Elementary School" in *Queering Elementary Education: Advancing the Dialogue about Sexualities and Schooling*, W. Letts and J. Sears, eds. Lanham, MD: Rowman & Littlefield Publishers, 1999.

———. *Troubling Education: Queer Activism and Anti-Oppressive Pedagogy*. New York: RoutledgeFalmer, 2002.

Lakoff, G., and M. Johnson. *Metaphors We Live By*. Chicago: University of Chicago Press, 1980.

Lamb, S. *The Secret Lives of Girls: What Good Girls Really Do—Sex Play, Aggression, and Their Guilt*. New York: Free Press, 2001.

Lancaster, R. *Sex Panic and the Punitive State*. Berkeley: University of California Press, 2011.

———. *The Trouble with Nature: Sex in Science and Popular Culture*. Berkeley: University of California Press, 2003.

Leavitt, R., and M. Power. "Civilizing Bodies: Children in Day Care" in *Making a Place for Pleasure in Early Childhood Education*, J. Tobin, ed. New Haven, CT: Yale University Press, 1997.

Lehr, V. *Queer Family Values: Debunking the Myth of the Nuclear Family*. Philadelphia: Temple University Press, 1999.

LeMoncheck, L., and M. Hajdin. *Sexual Harassment: A Debate*. Lanham, MD: Rowman & Littlefield Publishers, 1997.

Letts, W., and J. Sears, eds. *Queering Elementary Education: Advancing the Dialogue about Sexualities and Schooling*. Lanham, MD: Rowman & Littlefield Publishers, 1999.

Lev, A. *Transgender Emergence: Therapeutic Guidelines for Working with Gender-Variant People and Their Families*. New York: Routledge, 2004.

Levine, B. *Commonsense Rebellion: Taking Back Your Life from Drugs, Shrinks, Corporations, and a World Gone Crazy*. New York: Continuum, 2001.

Levine, J. *Harmful to Minors: The Perils of Protecting Children from Sex*. New York: Thunder's Mouth Press, 2003.

Lewis, B. *Moving Beyond Prozac, DSM, and the New Psychiatry: The Birth of Postpsychiatry*. Ann Arbor: The University of Michigan Press, 2009.

Lindemann, D. *Dominatrix: Gender, Eroticism, and Control in the Dungeon*. Chicago: University of Chicago Press, 2012.

Livingstone, T. "Anti-Sectarian, Queer, Client-Centeredness: A Re-iteration of Respect in Therapy" in *Counselling Ideologies: Queer Challenges to Heteronormativity*, L. Moon, ed. Farnham, UK: Ashgate, 2010.

Loe, M. *The Rise of Viagra: How the Little Blue Pill Changed Sex in America*. New York: New York University Press, 2004.

Lorde, A. *Sister Outsider*. Berkeley: Crossing Press, 2007.

Lynn, R. *The Sexual Revolution 2.0: Getting Connected, Upgrading Your Sex Life, and Finding True Love—or at Least a Dinner Date—in the Internet Age*. Berkeley: Ulysses Press, 2005.

Magnanti, B. *The Sex Myth: Why Everything We're Told Is Wrong*. London: Phoenix, 2013.

Mamo, L. *Queering Reproduction: Achieving Pregnancy in the Age of Technoscience*. Durham, NC and London: Duke University Press, 2007.

Marshall, E., and Ö. Sensoy. *Rethinking Popular Culture and Media*. Milwaukee: Rethinking Schools, 2011.

Martin, J. "The Crucial Place of Sexual Judgment for Field Theoretic Inquiries" in *Sexual Fields: Toward a Sociology of Collective Sexual Life*, A. Green, ed. Chicago: University of Chicago Press, 2014.

Martín-Baró, I. *Writings for a Liberation Psychology*. Cambridge, MA: Harvard University Press, 1994.

Martino, W., and M. Pallotta-Chiarolli. *So What's a Boy?: Addressing Issues of Masculinity and Schooling*. Buckingham, UK: Open University Press, 2003.

Matza, D. *Becoming Deviant*. Englewood Cliffs, NJ: Prentice Hall, 1969.

McCallum, E. L. *Object Lessons: How to Do Things with Fetishism*. Albany: State University of New York Press, 1999.

McGlotten, S. *Virtual Intimacies: Media, Affect, and Queer Sociality*. Albany: State University of New York Press, 2013.

McNair, B. *Porno? Chic!: How Pornography Changed the World and Made It a Better Place*. New York: Routledge, 2013.

McNamee, S., and K. Gergen. *Therapy as Social Construction*. London: Sage Publications, 1993.

McRuer, R. "Compulsory Able-bodiedness and Queer/Disabled Existence" in *Disability Studies: Enabling the Humanities*, S. Snyder, B. Brueggemann, and R. Garland-Thomson, eds. New York: Modern Language Association, 2002.

McRuer, R., and A. Mollow. *Sex and Disability*. Durham, NC and London: Duke University Press, 2012.

McRuer, R., and A. Wilkerson. "Desiring Disability: Queer Theory Meets Disability Studies," special issue, *Journal of Lesbian and Gay Studies* 9, no. 1/2 (2003). McWhorter, L. "Enemy of the Species" in *Queer Ecologies: Sex, Nature, Politics, Desire*, C. Mortimer-Sandilands and B. Erickson, eds. Bloomington: Indiana University Press, 2010.

Meiners, E., and T. Quinn, eds. *Sexualities in Education: A Reader*. New York: Peter Lang, 2012.

Meyer, E. "From Here to Queer: Mapping Sexualities in Education" in *Sexualities in Education: A Reader*, E. Meiners and T. Quinn, eds. New York: Peter Lang, 2012.

Middleton, S. *Disciplining Sexuality: Foucault, Life Histories, and Education*. New York: Teachers College Press, Columbia University, 1998.

Miller, J., J. Jordan, I. Stiver, M. Walker, J. Surrey, and N. Eldridge. "Therapists' Authenticity" in *The Complexity of Connection: Writings from the Stone Center's Jean Baker Miller Training Institute*. J. Jordan, M. Walker, and L. Hartling, eds. New York: The Guilford Press, 2004.

Mitchell, S. *Can Love Last?: The Fate of Romance over Time*. New York: W.W. Norton & Co., 2002.

Moane, G. *Gender and Colonialism: A Psychological Analysis of Oppression and Liberation*. New York: Palgrave Macmillan, 2011.

Mogul, J. L., A. J. Ritchie, and K. Whitlock. *Queer (In)justice: The Criminalization of LGBT People in the United States*. Boston: Beacon Press, 2011.

Moon, L, ed. *Counselling Ideologies: Queer Challenges to Heteronormativity*. Farnham, UK: Ashgate, 2010.

———. *Feeling Queer or Queer Feelings?: Radical Approaches to Counselling Sex, Sexualities and Genders*. London and New York: Routledge, 2008.

Morrow, R. "The Sexological Construction of Sexual Dysfunction." *Australian and New Zealand Journal of Sociology* 30 (1994): 20–35.

Mortimer-Sandilands, C., and B. Erickson, eds. *Queer Ecologies: Sex, Nature, Politics, Desire*. Bloomington: Indiana University Press, 2010.

Moser, C., and P. Kleinplatz. "DSM-IV-TR and the Paraphilias: An Argument for Removal." *Journal of Psychology & Human Sexuality* 17, no. 3/4 (2005): 91–109.

Moynihan, R., and B. Mintzes. *Sex, Lies, and Pharmaceuticals: How Drug Companies Plan to Profit from Female Sexual Dysfunction*. Vancouver: Greystone Books, 2010.

Mukhopadhyay, S. *Outdated: Why Dating Is Ruining Your Love Life*. Berkeley: Seal Press, 2011.

Muñoz, J. *Cruising Utopia: The Then and There of Queer Futurity.* New York: New York University Press, 2009.

Nelson, T. *The New Monogamy: Redefining Your Relationship After Infidelity*. Oakland, CA: New Harbinger Publications, Inc., 2012.

Nuñez, I. "Introduction: Teaching as Whole Self" in *Sexualities in Education: A Reader*, E. Meiners and T. Quinn, eds. New York: Peter Lang, 2012.

Ogas, O., and S. Gaddam. *A Billion Wicked Thoughts: What the World's Largest Experiment Reveals about Human Desire*. New York: Dutton, 2011.

Ogden, G. *The Return of Desire: A Guide to Rediscovering Your Sexual Passion*. Boston: Trumpeter Books, 2008.

O'Hara, S. "Talking with My Mouth Full" in *Policing Public Sex: Queer Politics and the Future of AIDS Activism*, Dangerous Bedfellows, eds. Boston: South End Press, 1996.

Ortmann, D., and R. Sprott. *Sexual Outsiders: Understanding BDSM Sexualities and Communities*. Lanham, MD: Rowman & Littlefield Publishers, 2013.

Paglia, C. *Vamps and Tramps: New Essays*. New York: Vintage Books, 1994.

Pallotta-Chiarolli, M. "'My Moving Days': A Child's Negotiation of Multiple Lifeworlds in Relation to Gender, Ethnicity, and Sexuality" in *Queering Elementary Education: Advancing the Dialogue about Sexualities and Schooling*, W. Letts and J. Sears, eds. Lanham, MD: Rowman & Littlefield Publishers, 1999.

Pappas, C. "Sex Sells, But What Else Does It Do? The American Porn Industry" in *Introducing the New Sexuality Studies*, 2nd ed., S. Seidman, N. Fisher, and C. Meeks, eds. New York: Routledge, 2011.

Parker, I., ed. *Deconstructing Psychotherapy*. London: Sage Publications, 1999.

Parker, R., and P. Aggleton. *Culture, Society, and Sexuality: A Reader*. London: UCL Press, 1999.

Patai, D. *Heterophobia: Sexual Harassment and the Future of Feminism*. Lanham, MD: Rowman & Littlefield Publishers, 2000.

Patton, C. *Sex and Germs: The Politics of AIDS*. Boston: South End Press, 1985.

Phillips, A. *Monogamy*. New York: Vintage Books, 1996.

Pitts-Taylor, V. *Surgery Junkies: Wellness and Pathology in Cosmetic Culture*. New Brunswick, NJ: Rutgers University Press, 2007.

Pollack, W. *Real Boys: Rescuing Our Sons from the Myths of Boyhood*. New York: Owl Books, 1998.

Pozner, J. *Reality Bites Back: The Troubling Truth about Guilty Pleasure TV*. Berkeley: Seal Press, 2010.

Preves, S. *Intersex and Identity: The Contested Self*. New Brunswick, NJ: Rutgers University Press, 2008.

Price, M. "Defining Mental Disability" in *The Disability Studies Reader*, 4th ed., L. Davis, ed. New York and London: Routledge, 2013.

Purkis, J., and J. Bowen. *Changing Anarchism: Anarchist Theory and Practice in a Global Age*. Manchester, UK, and New York: Manchester University Press, 2004.

Queen, C. *Exhibitionism for the Shy: Show Off, Dress Up, and Talk Hot*. San Francisco, CA: Down There Press, 2009.

Rambukkana, N. "Sex, Space, and Discourse: Non/Monogamy and Intimate Privilege in the Public Sphere" in *Understanding Non-Monogamies*, M. Barker and D. Langdridge, eds. New York: Routledge Press, 2010.

Rasmussen, M., E. Rofes, and S. Talburt, eds. *Youth and Sexualities: Pleasure, Subversion, and Insubordination in and out of School*. New York: Palgrave Macmillan, 2004.

Reavey, P. "When Past Meets Present to Produce a Sexual 'Other': Examining Professional and Everyday Narratives of Child Sexual Abuse and Sexuality" in *New Feminist Stories of Child Sexual Abuse: Sexual Scripts and Dangerous Dialogues*, P. Reavey and S. Warner, eds. New York: Routledge Press, 2003.

Reavey, P., and S. Warner, eds. *New Feminist Stories of Child Sexual Abuse: Sexual Scripts and Dangerous Dialogues*. New York: Routledge Press, 2003.

Redick, A. "Dangerous Practices: Ideological Uses of the 'Second Wave'" in *Policing Public Sex: Queer Politics and the Future of AIDS Activism*, Dangerous Bedfellows, eds. Boston: South End Press, 1996.

Reich, W. *Children of the Future: On the Prevention of Sexual Pathology*. New York: Farrar, Straus and Giroux, 1996.

Rice, F. P. *Intimate Relationships, Marriages, and Families*. Mountain View, CA: Mayfield Publishing, 1996.

Richardson, D. *Theorising Heterosexuality: Telling It Straight*. Philadelphia: Open University, 1998.

Richardson, S. "Sexes, Species, and Genomes: Why Males and Females Are Not Like Humans and Chimpanzees." *Biology and Philosophy* 25, no. 5 (2010): 823–841.

Richters, J. "Orgasm" in *Introducing the New Sexuality Studies*, S. Seidman, 2nd ed., S. Seidman, N. Fisher, and C. Meeks, eds. New York: Routledge, 2011.

Rind, B. "Pederasty: An Integration of Empirical, Historical, Sociological, Cross-Cultural, Cross-Species, and Evolutionary Evidence and Perspectives" in *Censoring Sex Research: The Debate over Male Intergenerational Relations*, T. Hubbard and B. Verstraete, eds. Walnut Creek, CA: Left Coast Press, 2013.

Rivera, M. "Linking the Psychological and the Social: Feminism, Poststructuralism, and Multiple Personality." *Dissociation* 2, no. 1 (1989): 24–31.

Rofes, E. *A Radical Rethinking of Sexuality and Schooling: Status Quo or Status Queer*. Lanham, MD: Rowman & Littlefield Publisher, 2005.

Roiphe, K. *The Morning After: Sex, Fear, and Feminism on Campus*. New York: Little, Brown, and Company, 1994.

Rose, J. *Sexuality in the Field of Vision*. London: Verso, 1986.

Rose, N. *Inventing Our Selves: Psychology, Power, and Personhood*. Cambridge, UK: Cambridge University Press, 1998.

———. *The Politics of Life Itself: Biomedicine, Power, and Subjectivity in the Twenty-First Century*. Princeton, NJ: Princeton University Press, 2007.

Roseneil, S. "Living and Loving Beyond the Heteronorm: A Queer Analysis of Personal Relationships in the Twenty-First Century." *Eurozine* online, May 29, 2007.

Roughgarden, J. *Evolution's Rainbow: Diversity, Gender, and Sexuality in Nature and People*. Los Angeles: University of California Press, 2013.

Rubin, G. "Thinking Sex: Notes for a Radical Theory of the Politics of Sexuality" in *Pleasure and Danger: Exploring Female Sexuality*, C. Vance, ed. Boston: Routledge & Kegan Paul, 1984.

Ryberg, I. "'Every Time We Fuck, We Win': The Public Sphere of Queer, Feminist, and Lesbian Porn as a (Safe) Space for Sexual Empowerment" in *The Feminist Porn Book: The Politics of Producing Pleasure*, T. Taormino, C. Shimizu, C. Penley, and M. Miller-Young, eds. New York: The Feminist Press, 2012.

Sandahl, C. "Queering the Crip or Cripping the Queer?: Intersections of Queer and Crip Identities in Solo Autobiographical Performance" in "Desiring Disability: Queer Theory Meets Disability Studies," R. McRuer and A. Wilkerson, eds., special issue, *Journal of Lesbian and Gay Studies* 9, no. 1/2 (2003): 25–56.

Savin-Williams, R. *The New Gay Teenager*. Cambridge, MA: Harvard University Press, 2005.

Schaef, A. *Co-Dependence: Misunderstood—Mistreated*. New York: Harper Collins, 1986.

Schalet, A. *Not Under My Roof: Parents, Teens, and the Culture of Sex*. Chicago: University of Chicago Press, 2011.

Schnarch, D. *Intimacy & Desire: Awaken the Passion in Your Relationship*. New York: Beaufort Books, 2009.

———. *Resurrecting Sex: Solving Sexual Problems & Revolutionizing Your Relationship*. New York: HarperCollins, 2002.

Schwartz, D. "Current Psychoanalytic Discourses on Sexuality: Tripping Over the Body" in *Disorienting Sexuality: Psychoanalytic Reappraisals of Sexual Identities*, T. Domenici and R. Lesser, eds. New York: Routledge Press, 1995.

Sears, J. "Teaching Queerly: Some Elementary Propositions" in *Queering Elementary Education: Advancing the Dialogue about Sexualities and Schooling*, W. Letts and J. Sears, eds. Lanham, MD: Rowman & Littlefield Publishers, 1999.

Segal, L. *New Sexual Agendas*. New York: New York University Press, 1997.

———. *Slow Motion: Changing Masculinities, Changing Men*. New Brunswick, NJ: Rutgers University Press, 1990.

Seidman, S. *Beyond the Closet: The Transformation of Gay and Lesbian Life*. New York: Routledge, 2002.

Seidman, S., N. Fischer, and C. Meeks, eds. *Introducing the New Sexualities Studies*, 2nd ed. New York: Routledge, 2011.

Serano, J. *Excluded: Making Feminist and Queer Movements More Inclusive*. Berkeley: Seal Press, 2013.

Silin, J. *Sex, Death, and the Education of Children: Our Passion for Ignorance in the Age of AIDS*. New York: Teachers College Press, Columbia University, 1995.

Slagle, R., and G. Yep. "Taming Brian: Sex, Love, and Romance in *Queer as Folk*" in *Critical Thinking About Sex, Love, and Romance in the Mass Media: Media Literacy Applications*, G. Galician and D. Merskin, eds. Mahwah, NJ: Lawrence Erlbaum Associates, 2007.

Spade, D. "About Purportedly Gendered Body Parts" on deanspade.net, February 3, 2011. Retrieved July 5, 2014.

Sprecher, S., and R. Cate. "Sexual Satisfaction and Sexual Expression as Predictors of Relationship Satisfaction and Stability" in *The Handbook of Sexuality in Close Relationships*, J. Harvey, A. Wenzel, and S. Sprecher, eds. Mahwah, NJ: Psychology Press, 2004.

Stacey, J. *In the Name of the Family: Rethinking Family Values in the Postmodern Age*. Boston: MA: Beacon Press, 1996.

Stafford, A. "Beyond Normalization: An Analysis of Heteronormativity in Children's Picture Books" in *Who's Your Daddy?: And Other Writings on Queer Parenting*, R. Epstein, ed. Toronto: Sumach Press, 2009.

Steinberg, D. "Technologies of Heterosexuality: Eugenic Reproductions Under Glass" in *Border Patrols: Policing the Boundaries of Heterosexuality*, D. Steinberg, D. Epstein, and R. Johnson, eds. London: Cassell, 1997.

Steinberg, D., D. Epstein, and R. Johnson, eds. *Border Patrols: Policing the Boundaries of Heterosexuality*. London: Cassell, 1997.

Stockton, K. *The Queer Child, or Growing Sideways in the Twentieth Century*. Durham, NC, and London: Duke University, 2009.

Stoller, R. *Presentations of Gender*. New Haven, CT: Yale University Press, 1985.

Strossen, N. *Defending Pornography: Free Speech, Sex, and the Fight for Women's Rights*. New York: New York University Press, 2000.

"Study Suggests 'Hookups' Can Turn into Meaningful Relationships." University of Iowa News Service. August 19, 2010. http://news-releases.uiowa.edu/2010/august/081910paik_relationships.html. Retrieved July 26, 2014.

Sturdivant, S. *Therapy with Women: A Feminist Philosophy of Treatment*. New York: Springer Publishing Company, 1980.

Sturgeon, N. *Environmentalism in Popular Culture: Gender, Race, Sexuality, and the Politics of the Natural*. Tucson: The University of Arizona Press, 2009.

———. "Penguin Family Values: The Nature of Planetary Environmental Reproductive Justice" in *Queer Ecologies: Sex, Nature, Politics, Desire*, C. Mortimer-Sandilands and B. Erickson, eds. Bloomington: Indiana University Press, 2010.

Szasz, T. *The Medicalization of Everyday Life: Selected Essays*. Syracuse, NY: Syracuse University Press, 2007.

———. *Sex by Prescription: The Startling Truth about Today's Sex Therapy*. Syracuse, NY: Syracuse University Press, 1980.

Tanenbaum, L. *Slut!: Growing Up Female with a Bad Reputation*. New York: Perennial, 2000.

Taormino, T., C. Shimizu, C. Penley, and M. Miller-Young, eds. *The Feminist Porn Book: The Politics of Producing Pleasure*. New York: The Feminist Press, 2012.

Tavris, C. *The Mismeasure of Woman: Why Women Are Not the Better Sex, the Inferior Sex, or the Opposite Sex*. New York: Touchstone, 1992.

Thomas, K. "Going Public: A Conversation with Lidell Jackson and Jocelyn Taylor" in *Policing Public Sex: Queer Politics and the Future of AIDS Activism*, Dangerous Bedfellows, eds. Boston: South End Press, 1996.

Thompson, J. B. *Ideology and Modern Culture: Critical Social Theory in the Era of Mass Communication*. Stanford, CA: Stanford University Press, 1990.

Tiefer, L. "Medicine, Morality and the Public Management of Sexual Matters" in *New Sexual Agendas*, L. Segal, ed. New York: New York University Press, 1997.

Tilsen, J. *Therapeutic Conversations with Queer Youth: Transcending Homonormativity and Constructing Preferred Identities*. Lanham, MD: Jason Aronson, 2013.

Tilsen, J., and D. Nylund. "Heteronormativity and Queer Youth Resistance: Reversing the Discourse" in *Counselling Ideologies: Queer Challenges to Heteronormativity*, L. Moon, ed. Farnham, UK: Ashgate, 2010.

Tisdale, S. *Talk Dirty to Me: An Intimate Philosophy of Sex*. New York: Anchor Books, 1994.

Tobin, J. *Making a Place for Pleasure in Early Childhood Education*. New Haven, CT: Yale University Press, 1997.

Traina, C. *Erotic Attunement: Parenthood and the Ethics of Sensuality between Unequals*. Chicago and London: University of Chicago Press, 2011.

Turkle, S. *Alone Together: Why We Expect More from Technology and Less from Each Other*. New York: Basic Books, 2011.

Ullerstam, L. *The Erotic Minorities*. New York: Grove Press, 1966.

Valenti, J. *The Purity Myth: How America's Obsession with Virginity Is Hurting Young Women*. Berkeley: Seal Press, 2010.

Vance, C. *Pleasure and Danger: Exploring Female Sexuality*. Boston: Routledge, 1984.

Walker, C. E. "Erotic Stimuli and the Aggressive Sexual Offender" in *Technical Report of the Commission on Obscenity and Pornography*, vol. 7. Washington, DC: US Government Printing Office, 1970.

Walker, N. "Throw Away the Master's Tools: Liberating Ourselves from the Pathology Paradigm." *Neurocosmopolitanism* (blog). August, 16, 2013. http://neurocosmopolitanism.com/throw-away-the-masters-tools-liberating-ourselves-from-the-pathology-paradigm/. Retrieved January 3, 2015.

Wallerstein, J., and S. Blakeslee. *The Good Marriage: How and Why Love Lasts*. New York: Houghton Mifflin, 1995.

Ward, J. "Queer Feminist Pigs: A Spectator's Manifesta" in *The Feminist Porn Book: The Politics of Producing Pleasure*, T. Taormino, C. Shimizu, C. Penley, and M. Miller-Young, eds. New York: The Feminist Press, 2012a.

———. "Tricky Adults and Bad Feelings." *Feminist Pigs* (blog). March 7, 2012b. http://feministpigs.blogspot.com/2012/03/tricky-adults-and-bad-feelings.html. Retrieved July 5, 2014.

Warner, S., and T. Wilkins. "Diagnosing Distress and Reproducing Disorder: Women, Child Sexual Abuse and Borderline Personality Disorder" in *New Feminist Stories of Child Sexual Abuse: Sexual Scripts and Dangerous Dialogues*, P. Reavey and S. Warner, eds. New York: Routledge Press, 2003.

Watkins, M., and H. Shulman. *Toward Psychologies of Liberation: Critical Theory and Practice in Psychology and the Human Sciences*. Basingstroke, UK: Palgrave Macmillan, 2008.

Watters, E. *Crazy Like Us: The Globalization of the American Psyche*. New York: Free Press, 2010.

Watters, E., and R. Ofshe. *Therapy's Delusions: The Myth of the Unconscious and the Exploitation of Today's Walking Worried*. New York: Scribner, 1999.

Weiner Davis, M. *The Sex-Starved Marriage: Boosting Your Marriage Libido*. New York: Simon & Schuster, 2003.

Wilkerson, A. "Disability, Sex Radicalism, and Political Agency" in *Feminist Disability Studies*, K. Hall, ed. Bloomington: Indiana University Press, 2011.

Winnubst, S. *Queering Freedom*. Bloomington, IN: Indiana University Press, 2006.

Yates, A. *Sex Without Shame: Encouraging the Child's Healthy Sexual Development*. New York: Quill, 1982.

Zeitner, R. *Self Within Marriage: The Foundation for Lasting Relationships*. New York: Routledge, 2012.

INDEX

G

N

O

P

S